SOCIAL EDUCATION

TEXT AND COURSEWORK BOOK

for

Leaving Certificate Applied

3rd Edition

EILIS FLOOD

g GILL EDUCATION

Gill Education

Hume Avenue, Park West, Dublin 12

www.gilleducation.ie

Gill Education is an imprint of M.H. Gill & Co.

978 07171 4517 1

Print origination in Ireland by O'K Graphic Design, Dublin

The paper used in this book is made from the wood pulp of managed forests. For every tree felled, at least one tree is planted, thereby renewing natural resources.

Picture Credits

For permission to reproduce photographs and other material, the author and publisher gratefully acknowledge the following:

THE ADVERTISING ARCHIVE: 41; ALAMY: 2, 4, 4, 5, 7, 28T, 28C, 33, 35, 38, 39, 48BL, 48BC, 48BR, 51T, 61, 68BL, 76BL, 104, 106TL, 106TC, 106TR, 111CR, 131CL, 218, 270, 272; AWARE: 195CR; BARNARDOS: 195CL; CHILDLINE: 195TR; CREDIT UNION: 266, 277; CURA: 195TL, 214TC; ENCAMS: 111CL; FIANNA FÁIL: 225; FINE GAEL: 225; GETTY: 30, 77, 133, 141, 142, 161, 212; GREEN PARTY: 225; IMAGEFILE: 5, 36, 51C, 67, 76BR, 97, 111T, 125, 190; LABOUR: 224; LASER: 273; OIREACHTAS: 226; PA PHOTOS: 65, 98, 131CR; REUTERS: 219, 224; THE SAMARITANS: 214TR; SCIENCE PHOTO LIBRARY: 68BR; SINN FÉIN: 225; ST. VINCENT DE PAUL: 214TL; UNITED NATIONS: 131T; WOMENS AID: 209.

The author and publisher have made every effort to trace all copyright holders, but if any has been inadvertently overlooked we would be pleased to make the necessary arrangements at the first opportunity.

Acknowledgments

Thanks to VHI Healthcare for permission to use the podcast 'Binge drinking – Addiction or Social norm'.

Contents

Introduction to the Course   v

Module 1   **Social and Health Education 1**   1
  Unit 1   Self and Others   2
  Unit 2   Taking Care of Yourself   11
  Unit 3   Relationships and Sexuality   54

Module 2   **My Community**   79
  Unit 1   Research Skills   80
  Unit 2   My Own Place   88
  Unit 3   My Family in the Local Area   95
  Unit 4   My Own Place in the Past   96
  Unit 5   Community Amenities/Resources   99
  Unit 6   Planning in My Own Place   106

Module 3   **Contemporary Issues 1**   113
  Unit 1   Social Context of Contemporary Issues   114
  Unit 2   Forces/Interests   116
  Unit 3   Making Links   120
  Unit 4   Contemporary Issues and Human Rights   125
  Unit 5   Making Connections   134
  Unit 6   Understanding Concepts   137

Module 4   **Social and Health Education 2**   147
  Unit 1   Communication   148
  Unit 2   Relationships   157
  Unit 3   Coping with Problems   173

Module 5   **Contemporary Issues 2**   197
  Unit 1   Influences on Contemporary Issues: The Media   198
  Unit 2   Influences on Contemporary Issues: Interest Groups   209
  Unit 3   Democratic Institutions   214

Unit 4	Active Citizenship: Voting/The Budget	226
Unit 5	Civil Rights and Responsibilities	235
Unit 6	Contemporary Issue Task	244
Module 6	**Taking Charge**	**251**
Unit 1	A Place of My Own	252
Unit 2	Making Ends Meet	263
Unit 3	Account Options	265
Unit 4	Saving and Borrowing	278
Unit 5	Buying My Own Home	281
Unit 6	Understanding Insurance	287

Introduction to the Course

It is very important when we start something new that we set goals for ourselves. This means that we should think about why we are doing the new thing and what we hope to gain through doing it. You are starting a totally new subject, which none of you will have studied before. Therefore, before considering your goals, find out some basic information about this course:

ACTIVITY

- What is the name of this subject? _____
- List the six modules in this course.

1. _____
2. _____
3. _____
4. _____
5. _____
6. _____

When you complete each Social Education module successfully you can claim one credit. What do you need to do to claim your credit at the end of each module? The first answer has been done for you, and you have been given a clue to the others.

1. I must take part as best I can in all class activities.

2. (Something about key assignments.) I must . . .

_____
_____
_____

3. (Something about attendance.) I must . . .

_____
_____
_____

Module ONE

Social and Health Education 1

This module should be completed during sessions 1 and 2 (throughout Year 1) of the LCA Social Education Course.

Below are the four key assignments for Module 1. You must do ALL of them. As you work through this module and complete each assignment, come back to this page and tick it off.

1. I completed exercises and work sheets on assertive, aggressive and passive behaviour and different communication styles.

   Date: ___ /___ /_____

2. I collected information on healthy lifestyles and made a plan to improve one aspect of my own lifestyle.

   Date: ___ /___ /_____

3. As a member of a small group, I collected information from magazines and newspapers and used it to make a collage illustrating ways in which the media promote sex-stereotyping.

   Date: ___ /___ /_____

4. I presented a report on a drug in which I described five things that I learned about the drug, its effects and the risks involved in taking it.

   Date: ___ /___ /_____

UNIT 1 Self and Others

Listening Skills

Have you ever found yourself talking to someone and getting the feeling that they were not listening? How did you know that they were not listening? How did it make you feel? We need to listen to people when they talk to us, for a number of reasons. Two of these are:

- it is polite to listen to people;
- we can get the information we need if we listen.

Effective Communication

Effective communication occurs when a message of some sort is passed between two or more people. Speech may or may not be part of effective communication. Active listening is part of effective communication. The rules of effective communication are:

- Speak clearly.
- Keep good eye contact, both when you are speaking and when you are listening to others.
- Do not interrupt except to ask questions or if you want more information or do not fully understand.
- Sometimes we nod or say things like 'yes' or 'right', which shows we are listening.

Body Language and Gleaning Details

It is estimated that between 55 and 65 per cent of what we communicate to others does not involve words at all, but instead involves our body language. Look at the table below outlining what different body language signs can mean.

Body language sign	What sign may communicate to others
Hands • Hiding hands • Nail biting	• Secretive, possibly lying • Nervous, lacking in self confidence
Handshakes • Limp • Firm • Double handshake	• Nervous, disinterested, lacking in confidence • Confident and friendly • Very confident and friendly, mini-embrace, invitation to trust (only used if you know the person well)

Eyes – 'The window of the soul'

• Staring	• Aggression
• Glazed over, often with arching brows	• Bored, sleepy, uninterested
• Good eye contact	• Interest
• Glancing repeatedly at someone in the distance	• Attraction
• Avoiding eye contact	• Shyness, lack of confidence, lying, guilt
• Slow blinking	• Sleepy, loss of interest
• Excessive blinking	• Stress, lying, showing romantic interest
• Rolling eyes upwards	• Disbelief, disagreement

Mouth

• Whole face smile (teeth shown, cheeks rise and eyes crinkle)	• Genuine smile
• Closed lips smile	• Fake smile – or person may be embarrassed by teeth
• Covering the mouth when smiling	• Low self-confidence, may be embarrassed by teeth
• Closed mouth, tight jaw muscles	• Aggression
• Pursed lips	• Aggression, disagreement
• Lip biting	• Nervous

Head

• Fiddling with hair	• Nervous: some women = flirting tool
• Fiddling with ears, rubbing the face/chin	• Nervousness, anxiety
• Ears reddening	• Can indicate lying
• Tilted head	• Paying attention
• Nodding	• Shows interest and agreement (note: in some countries, e.g. Bulgaria and India, nodding the head actually means 'no')

Legs and arms

• Crossed arms	• Defensive – something to hide, uninviting
• Touching someone's arm	• Sympathy, trust
• Crossed legs or ankles	• Nervous, ill at ease
• Ankle crossed over knee (mostly men)	• Confidence, arrogance
• Uncrossed legs	• Open to communication
• Jiggling or tapping foot	• Nervous or bored

Your body language can give either a good or a bad impression.

Imagine you are at an interview.
List three body language signs you would avoid.

1. _____
2. _____
3. _____

List five body language signs you would use.

1. _____
2. _____
3. _____
4. _____
5. _____

Gleaning details

As human beings we frequently make quick, often stereotypical, judgements about the people around us. We make these judgements using what are called 'gleaning details'. Examples of gleaning details are particular hairstyles, clothes, posture, body movements and accents. Look at the pictures opposite. Which group do you think would be judged as having the most money? Which group do you think are most likely to be judged as being at university or college? Which group do you think are most likely to be judged as smokers? Which group are most likely to be judged as binge drinkers? Which group do you think is most likely to be judged as having good health? Which group is most likely to be judged as being likely to be in trouble with the law? What gleaning details do you think judgements are made on?

When people go to an interview they may be judged very quickly by their body language and also their gleaning details. It is therefore very important to be aware of and avoid gleaning details and body language that give the wrong impression.

Examples of gleaning details to avoid:

- Wearing tracksuits or revealing clothes.
- Having tattoos showing.
- Very obviously dyed hair, e.g. peroxide blonde with roots showing.
- Wearing a lot of jewellery.
- Wearing a lot of make-up.
- Smoking before the interview (the people on the panel will be able to smell it).

KEY ASSIGNMENT

Effective communication

In the spaces below list four guidelines to effective communication. This exercise can go towards partial completion of the first key assignment for this module.

1. _____

2. _____

3. _____

4. _____

Me! I am a Positive Person

 ACTIVITY

Create a collage which illustrates your long-term goals for the future. You could call your collage 'Me in 10 years' time'. Use magazine cuttings, drawings of your own, etc.

Talk about your collage with the rest of the group afterwards.

 **ACTIVITY**

Fill out the 'work card' below with information about yourself.

My name is: _____

My date of birth is: _____

When I leave school I want to be a: _____

A TV programme I like is: _____

A film I like is: _____

A song I like is: _____

One thing I like about school/youthreach is: _____

_____

One thing I like about the weekend is: _____

My favourite dinner is: _____

The thing that scares me most is: _____

_____

I get nervous when: _____

_____

My opinions

People who litter: _____

_____

Legalisation of cannabis: _____

_____

Homosexuality: _____

_____

Three good things about myself are:

1. _____

2. _____

3. _____

If I had to name one thing that I've done that

I am proud of it would be: _____

_____

If I could change one thing about myself it would be: _____

_____

I am an Intelligent, Capable Person!

In the past, many people took a very narrow view of intelligence, seeing it only in terms of passing written exams and tests. Nowadays it is generally accepted that intelligence is much broader than this, and that there is such a thing as multiple intelligence: you may not be good at exams but instead have some other skill or ability that is of value to society. Think, for example, of soccer players, musicians, or tradespeople.

Society now values different forms of intelligence

 **ACTIVITY**

How good are you at the following things? (Please tick)

Activity	Excellent	Good	Not very good
Sport			
Singing			
Playing an instrument			
Painting			
Looking after children			
Talking to people			
Cooking			
Keeping myself and my surroundings tidy			
Telling jokes			
Recognising songs after only a few notes			
Guessing how long something is			
Adding in my head			

Seven Intelligences

In a primary school, a ten-year-old boy is having difficulty reading a book designed for a six-year-old. When the bell rings he goes out to play football. He is easily the best player in the school: he does not even have to think about what he is going to do with the ball because he just instinctively knows. Another girl is inside trying to correct her maths homework. She tries hard at maths but never seems to be able to get it right. But she is brilliant at art. She can paint and draw anything you could ask for. Both of these children show clear signs of intelligence, yet neither of them might score very highly on an IQ test. Individuals like this demonstrate that there are many different types of intelligence, most of which cannot be measured by the usual tests. It is believed that there are perhaps seven different forms of intelligence:

1.	Language	People who are good at telling or writing stories, telling jokes, or songwriting.
2.	Logic and maths	People who can fix things, make things out of wood and metal, estimate the weight or length of something, etc.
3.	Visual and spatial thinking	People who are good at art, sculpture, photography, fashion, interior decorating, gardening.
4.	Music	People who can play music, sing, write music.
5.	Bodily (kinaesthetic)	People who can dance or play sports well.
6.	Intrapersonal skills	People who have a good self-knowledge.
7.	Interpersonal skills	People who get along well with others or have good leadership skills.

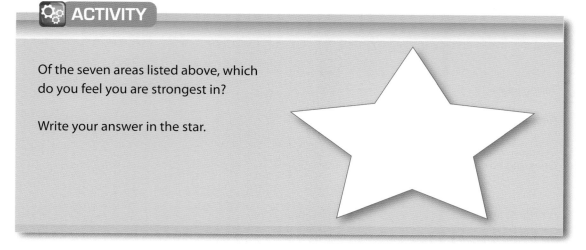

ACTIVITY

Of the seven areas listed above, which do you feel you are strongest in?

Write your answer in the star.

Passive, Assertive and Aggressive Behaviour

Being assertive is believing that you have the right to ask for what you want and need. It is closely linked to having high self-esteem or feeling good about yourself. Not everyone finds it easy to be assertive.

Some people behave passively, and do not tell others clearly what their wants and needs are. They are afraid of making enemies and so try to please everyone.

The opposite of passive is aggressive. People who behave aggressively try to bully others into getting what they want.

 KEY ASSIGNMENT

Key Assignment: Assertive, aggressive and passive behaviour

In this activity you are given a number of sample situations, and a possible response to each one. Write in the oval space whether you think the response is passive, aggressive or assertive.

Situation 1

A teacher wrongly accuses you of copying in a test.

Response: You say you didn't, and ask to speak to the teacher after class so that you can explain your case calmly and fully without the whole class listening.

Situation 2

You have bought a new outfit that you really like. Some of the others in your class make fun of it, saying it's something their mother would wear.

Response: You are confident about how the outfit looks and say that it would be a pity if we all had the same taste; the world would be a very boring place.

Situation 3

You are in a fast food restaurant and order a burger and chips. When the food eventually comes it is cold and very greasy.

Response: You do nothing and throw the burger and chips away without eating them.

In each of the above situations, write down what you think your usual response would be, and whether you consider this response to be passive, assertive or aggressive.

Situation 1: _____

_____

Situation 2: _____

_____

Situation 3: _____

_____

Roleplays

Divide into pairs. Each pair picks one of the above situations. Think about what the assertive response would be. If you like, practise roleplaying this response and then come back and present it to the whole group.

📄 EXAM TIME

Social Education (2006) – short questions

1. An assertive person is someone who:

   Asks for what he/she wants and needs in a direct and clear manner

   Forces people to do what he/she wants and never backs down

   Remains silent as he/she does not want to offend others

Social Education (2008) – short questions

2. Which of the following is an assertive way of dealing with a conflict situation?

   Ignore the situation until the problem is solved

   Hit first, ask questions later

   State your position clearly and calmly

UNIT 2 Taking Care of Yourself

The World Health Organisation (WHO) describes health as:

> *A complete state of physical, mental and social well-being and not simply the absence of disease or infirmity.*

ACTIVITY

Discuss this definition of health in class and come up with six factors that contribute to a healthy lifestyle and therefore good health.

1. _____
2. _____
3. _____
4. _____
5. _____
6. _____

List six things that contribute to an unhealthy lifestyle and therefore bad health. Remember! Health means mental and social as well as physical well-being.

1. _____
2. _____
3. _____
4. _____
5. _____
6. _____

Stress and its Management

What is stress?

Stress is a normal response that occurs when we experience or think we will experience difficulties in our lives. Stress is both physical and mental. Sometimes the cause of stress can be a one-off problem and be relatively short term, e.g. when moving house, changing schools or taking exams. At other times stress can be ongoing or long term, e.g. living with parents who are heavy drinkers or being bullied at school. Both types of stress are unpleasant and difficult to cope with, but because the second type is ongoing it can be the most damaging.

It is generally accepted that the stress response occurs in three stages.

Stage 1

The body becomes alarmed because it recognises that a situation is unpleasant.

A chemical hormone called adrenaline is released by the body. This hormone is called the 'fight or flight' hormone and was very important for the survival of our ancestors as they had to run away from wild animals and other dangers.

Stage 2

If the cause of the stress goes away, the body can restore itself to normal. This is the second stage and is called resistance.

Stage 3

If the cause of stress does not go away, however, the body stays in an alarmed state and eventually becomes exhausted. This is Stage 3. It is when a person reaches Stage 3 that mental and physical health problems arise.

Common effects of stress on the body

Short term	Long term
increased heartbeat	frequent headaches
faster breathing	backache
sweating	asthma
indigestion	high blood pressure
anxiety	reduced ability to fight infections

Common effects on mental well-being

• tension	• frustration and anger
• being easily irritated	• tiredness
• feeling bad about yourself (*low self-esteem*)	• being depressed
	• high blood pressure
	• being tearful
	• feeling unable to cope

Stressors

 **ACTIVITY**

Things that cause stress are called 'stressors'. In today's society there are a huge number of stressors. Can you write down three things or situations that cause some amount of stress in your life?

1. _____

2. _____

3. _____

Stress and personality type

Have you ever noticed that some people seem to spend their lives looking stressed and others go through life as if they haven't a care in the world? It is thought that whether you get easily stressed or not depends largely on your personality type. There are basically two personality types:

Type A = gets stressed easily
Type B = doesn't get stressed easily

Type A personalities are always pushing themselves and are very competitive. They are not happy unless they are the best at whatever they decide to do. Type A personalities need frequent praise and recognition. They are always rushing against the clock and are sometimes irritable and unreasonable. They tend to suffer more from stress and stress-related illnesses.

Type B personalities, on the other hand, are sometimes thought of as being lazy. They do not really push themselves and rarely do more than enough to get through. They are not very competitive and do not get upset if others achieve more than they do. Type B personalities like praise but do not go looking for it. They avoid confrontation with others at all costs.

Note: Type A and Type B are fairly extreme; many people fall somewhere between the two personality types.

ACTIVITY

What personality type are you?	Yes	No
1. Does it annoy you when a teacher is slow to give back corrected work?	☐	☐
2. Would you know what mark others in your class got in a test?	☐	☐
3. Would you borrow money to buy brand name clothes?	☐	☐
4. Do you generally walk quickly?	☐	☐
5. Do you often eat while standing up?	☐	☐
6. Are you often late for things?	☐	☐
7. If a friend wanted to go out and you didn't, would you go anyway?	☐	☐
8. Do you find it difficult to sit still in class?	☐	☐
9. When you are eating a packet of sweets do you chew more than one at a time?	☐	☐
10. When you are getting ready to go out, do you try on several outfits before choosing what to wear?	☐	☐
11. Do you get heartburn frequently?	☐	☐
12. Do you get headaches frequently?	☐	☐
13. Do you get very nervous before a test?	☐	☐
14. Do you fidget a lot?	☐	☐
15. Do you bite your nails?	☐	☐

Count the number of yes and no answers you had. Write the results below.

Yes answers ____   No answers ____

If you had 10-15 'yes' answers you seem to have a 'type A' personality. If you had 10-15 'no' answers you seem to have a 'type B' personality. If you have roughly 7-8 of each you are in between.

People need a certain amount of stress to stay alert and interested in their lives. If we are under-stressed we will not be enthusiastic in our work, and we will be frequently bored or even depressed.

Stress management

Stress is an unfortunate but unavoidable part of modern life. Stress, as we have already seen, is very dangerous if it is not managed properly. Some people manage their stress very badly or not at all. They:

- overeat
- drink too much
- smoke too much
- take drugs
- avoid going to work or school if this is where the stress is
- stay out late if the stress is at home.

People who try to cope with stress in these ways eventually exhaust themselves and burn out. Luckily there are other, much better ways of dealing with stress in our lives.

The first step to good stress management is to accept that there is a problem (or problems) in your life that are causing you stress. You must then decide what to do about them.

You have two basic choices:

1.   Try to get rid of the cause of the stress (the problem).

2.   Try to cope effectively with the symptoms of stress.

Take this example:
Some people in your class will not sit beside you because they say you smell.
This causes you stress.
What can you do? You can get rid of the problem by washing your clothes and yourself every day.
However, not all problems can be solved like this.

Take this example:

You have come to live in Ireland from England and have to study Irish as part of your LCA. You get very stressed when you have Irish class as it is too difficult and everyone knows more than you. You cannot avoid the problem, i.e. by missing class every day, so you must learn to deal with the problem in other ways.

Some ways of coping with stress are:

- Talking to a trusted friend about your problem.
- Exercise, e.g. walking or playing a physical game.
- Breathing or other relaxation exercises.
- OLGA – a coping mechanism.

Breathing techniques

When you feel stressed, e.g. at the start of an exam, try this breathing technique.

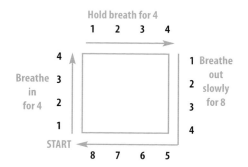

 CD - Track 1

Relaxation exercise
Listen to Track 1 and carry out the relaxation exercise as you listen.

OLGA

OLGA is a way of dealing with stress in three simple stages:

Stage 1 – O

OBSERVE what is happening to you. For example, you are worried that some of the girls/boys in your year are talking behind your back, making fun of you. You are in class thinking about this and it is driving you mad, it is causing you a lot of stress.

Stage 2 – LG

LET GO – realise that there is nothing you can do about it at this point in time.

Stage 3 – A

ATTEND – to what you are meant to be doing. Put the thoughts of what they may be saying away and concentrate on what you should be doing now, i.e. your classwork.

🄲 CD - Track 2

Listen to Track 2 and answer the questions. Fiona is 17. She is a bright young girl who is being bullied by a group of girls at school.

The ringleader is a girl called Sonya, who is not very good at school. Sonya and her gang bully Fiona in a very subtle, yet cruel way. Fiona has started to miss school regularly because of it.

Her year head, Ms Browne, has noticed this and talks to Fiona about it.

1. What causes Fiona to experience stress?

    _____

    _____

2. Sonya and her gang bully Fiona in a very subtle, yet cruel way. What do you think this means?

    _____

    _____

3. Why do you think people bully?

    _____

    _____

4. How does Fiona try to cope with the stress?

    _____

    _____

5. Is her stress management effective? If not, what could she do instead?

    _____

    _____

Good Nutrition

Healthy eating is very important for you to look well and feel well. No face creams or health supplements can take the place of eating a wide variety of fresh foods and drinking plenty of fresh clean water. Most of us have some idea of what we should and should not be eating, but for a lot of people working out a balanced diet for themselves seems too complicated and too much like hard work! The food pyramid in the diagram is designed to take the hard work out of planning a healthy, balanced diet for a teenager. (Note: you should drink approximately eight glasses of water every day.)

What is a serving?

Bread, cereals and potato group	Fruit and vegetable group	Milk, cheese and yoghurt group	Meat, fish, eggs and meat alternative group
1 bowl of cereal 1 slice of bread 4 dessertspoons of rice/pasta 1 potato	1/2 glass fruit juice 4 dessertspoons cooked vegetables 1 bowl homemade vegetable soup 1 piece fresh fruit 4 dessertspoons of cooked or tinned fruit 12 dessertspoons peas/beans	1 glass milk 1 carton yoghurt 1 matchbox-sized piece of cheese	50g red meat/chicken 75g fish 2 eggs 75g nuts 75g TVP

If a person has trouble with their diet, for example if they are very over- or underweight, they can go to the hospital to see a dietician. The dietician would try to get an idea of what sort of eating habits the person has by doing a 24-hour recall. This means that the dietician finds out and writes down exactly what the person eats and drinks in a given 24-hour period. Below is a 24-hour recall chart for you to fill out. It is not as complicated as a real one, but it will give you a general picture of your eating habits.

 ACTIVITY

24-hour recall

What did you eat yesterday? Write down everything, including sweets, drinks, etc. Be as accurate as you can, for example write 'two slices of bread', not just 'bread'.

Date of 24-hour recall ___/___/___

Breakfast	Mid-morning break
Lunch	Mid-afternoon break
Dinner	Supper

Evaluate your eating habits:

In general do you think your diet is a healthy one?   Yes   No

What   foods   should   you   increase?

_____

_____

What foods should you reduce? _____

🔍 KEY ASSIGNMENT

Using the knowledge that you have gained as a result of studying the food pyramid, plan out a daily menu for yourself.

(This activity will fulfil the first part of your Key Assignment 2.)

When you have completed the second part of this key assignment, go to page 1 and tick off Assignment 2 on the checklist.

Daily Menu

Breakfast: **Mid-afternoon break:**

Mid-morning break: **Evening dinner:**

Lunch: **Supper:**

Safe Alcohol Limits

Fully grown men: 21 units per week (no more than 6–8 in one night)

Fully grown women: 14 units per week (no more than 4–6 in one night)

| 1 unit glass of lager, cider or beer | 2 units pint of lager, cider or beer | 1 unit small glass of wine | 1 unit shot of spirits | 1½ units ready-mixed drink, alcopops, e.g. WKD |

ACTIVITY

What is a unit?

1. On Sunday night Peter drank five pints and a vodka and coke.
   How many units did he consume? _____
   Is he within recommended limits?   Yes ▨   No ▨

2. On Saturday night Eoin drank three pints of cider.

   How many units did he consume? _____

   Is he within recommended limits?   Yes ▨   No ▨

3. On Monday night Samantha drank four glasses of lager.

   How many units did she consume? _____

   Is she within recommended limits?   Yes ▨   No ▨

4. On Saturday night Anna drank five ready-mixed alcopops.

   How many units did she consume? _____

   Is she within recommended limits?   Yes ▨   No ▨

Binge drinking

CD - Track 3

Listen to Track 3 on binge drinking and answer the questions below.

1. Ireland has the highest percentage of teenage binge drinkers in Europe.
                                True ▨   False ▨

2. What percentage of Irish people are estimated to suffer from alcoholism?

   _____

3. List three effects of hangovers mentioned by the young people speaking on the recording.

   a) _____

   b) _____

   c) _____

4. According to Stephen Rowen how does the World Health Organisation define binge drinking?

   _____

5. Name two 'high-risk' behaviours that are frequently associated with binge drinking.

   a) _____

   b) _____

6. List two long-term effects associated with binge drinking.

   a) _____

   b) _____

7. Why, according to the recording, has there been an increase in teenage binge drinking in recent years?

   _____

   _____

   _____

8. If you suspect that you or someone close to you has a problem with alcohol, what can you do?

   _____

   _____

   _____

Exercise and Fitness

Exercise, like eating well, is something that is very important if we are to feel and look good. Young children don't need to be told to take exercise. It is usually when children turn into young adults that some may stop taking regular exercise. During the teenage years patterns are established that may stay with you for life. This is why it is important to take regular exercise when you go into secondary school and keep it up even when you leave school.

ACTIVITY

Below are a list of reasons why people take regular exercise.
Tick whether each reason is important to you or not.

To keep fit	Yes	No
To look well	Yes	No
To meet lots of people	Yes	No
To build up and keep good bone density	Yes	No
I like it	Yes	No
To release stress	Yes	No

To prevent heart disease	Yes	No	
To keep my lungs healthy and strong	Yes	No	
To keep my weight down	Yes	No	
I like winning	Yes	No	
Sport is my talent	Yes	No	

 **ACTIVITY**

Survey of exercise habit
Why not find out how much exercise others in your school or centre take each week? You could do this by getting them to fill out a questionnaire like the one opposite. When you have the questionnaires filled out, present your results using bar charts, etc.

Rest, Relaxation and Sleep

Rest, relaxation and sleep are vital to good health as this is how the body re-energises itself. It is recommended that you get at least eight hours' sleep every night.

ACTIVITY

Starting next Monday, monitor the number of hours' sleep you get for the whole week and record your findings below. Add all the hours together and divide by seven to get the average number of hours' sleep that you had per night.

Monday night	_____	Tuesday night	_____
Wednesday night	_____	Thursday night	_____
Friday night	_____	Saturday night	_____
Sunday night	_____		

Average per night _____

REGULAR EXERCISE QUESTIONNAIRE

1. Are you male or female? _____

2. Approximately how much free time did you have in the last 24 hours? _____

3. Which of these activities do you do most in your free time? (pick one)

A. Watch TV or videos	☐	E. Listen to music	☐
B. Play computer games	☐	F. Sleep	☐
C. Read books/magazines	☐	G. Play sports	☐
D. Go into town with friends	☐	H. Meet my boy/girlfriend	☐

4. Would you describe yourself as a physically active individual? Yes ☐ No ☐

5. Tick the exercise you take most often. How often do you take part in this activity? (E.g. twice a week, etc.)

A. Walking	☐ _____	E. Basketball	☐ _____
B. Football	☐ _____	F. Camogie	☐ _____
C. Jogging	☐ _____	G. Dancing	☐ _____
D. Swimming	☐ _____	H. Other	☐ _____

6. Do you think exercise is important?   Yes ☐   No ☐

7. Tick any of the reasons below that are important to you.

   A. It keeps my heart and lungs healthy. ☐

   B. It keeps my weight down. ☐

   C. It keeps me out of trouble. ☐

   D. I would be bored if I didn't take exercise. ☐

   E. I meet people through sport/exercise. ☐

   F. I enjoy it. ☐

   G. Sport is my best talent. ☐

Name one physical activity that you will participate in next week.

_____

Psychological Well-Being

Psychological or mental well-being is another essential ingredient for good health. The following are necessary to achieve this. Discuss what each one means with your teacher and the rest of the group.

- positive self image
- a sense of belonging
- a sense of security and safety
- fun and enjoyment.

Drugs

What is a drug?

A drug is a substance (with the exception of food) that changes:

- how the body works
- how a person acts
- how a person feels
- how a person thinks.

Category	General effects	Examples
Sedatives	Relief of tension/anxiety. Sleep-inducing. Physical and psychological dependence.	Sleeping tablets, tranquillisers e.g. Valium, cannabis.
Hallucinogens	Cause changes in mood and thought patterns. Person may see/hear things not really there. Bad trips, flashbacks.	LSD, magic mushrooms, Ecstasy, cannabis.
Depressants	Slow down nervous system, making person more relaxed but co-ordination affected.	Alcohol.
Opiates	Cause feelings of euphoria but physically and psychologically addictive.	Heroin, methadone, morphine.
Stimulants	Increase heart and breathing rates. Prevents sleep. Fluid loss.	Caffeine, nicotine, Ecstasy, cocaine.

Most countries try to stop the use of dangerous drugs by banning or limiting their use. Countries do this for the following reasons:

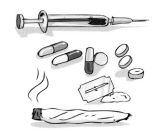

- health promotion (e.g. government warnings on cigarettes)
- protection of others (e.g. drink driving laws)
- keeping law and order (e.g. to stop addicts stealing to feed their habit).

⚙ ACTIVITY

1. List all the reasons you can think of why a young person might decide to get involved in drugs.

   _____

   _____

   _____

2. List all the reasons you can think of why a young person might decide not to get involved in drugs.

   _____

   _____

   _____

3. 'Frequently drug addicts blame things like coming from a bad area, unemployment and family problems for getting involved with drugs in the first place. Some people think it is time they stopped blaming everyone else and started taking responsibility for their own behaviour.'
   Discuss this statement with your class group. Write down what you think below.

   _____

   _____

   _____

Smoking

Over the years many thousands of euros have been spent by the government in an effort to stop people smoking. Some people think that this money has been largely wasted, believing that there are as many people smoking today as ever. It is illegal to buy cigarettes if you are under 18 years of age.

⚙ ACTIVITY

Your group could carry out a piece of research on smoking in your school/centre by asking other classes to fill out a questionnaire like the one on the next page. Present your results using pie charts, bar charts, etc.

SMOKING QUESTIONNAIRE

1. Are you: Male ☐   Female ☐

2. Are you over 18?   Yes ☐   No ☐

3. Do you smoke?   Yes ☐   No ☐

   If yes, on average how many cigarettes do you smoke per day?

   0–5 ☐   5–10 ☐   10-15 ☐   15-20 ☐   more ☐

4. Do you know how much a packet of cigarettes costs?

                                                    Yes ☐   No ☐

   If yes, how much? _____

5. Why do you smoke? You can tick more than one.

   (Leave blank if you do not smoke.)

   A.   Cigarettes make me feel more confident.   ☐

   B.   Smoking calms me.   ☐

   C.   All my friends smoke.   ☐

   D.   I am addicted.   ☐

   F.   No good reason.   ☐

6. Attitudes to smoking – what do you think?

		Agree	Don't know	Disagree
A.	The bad effects of smoking are exaggerated.	☐	☐	☐
B.	Smoking is a filthy habit.	☐	☐	☐
C.	Quitting smoking is very difficult.	☐	☐	☐
D.	Banning smoking in all public places is a good thing.	☐	☐	☐
E.	Smoking has a glamorous image.	☐	☐	☐
F.	Smoking will affect my health.	☐	☐	☐
G.	It is easy to tell from their appearance if a person smokes or not.	☐	☐	☐

7. In years to come, if your children started smoking, what would you do?

   _____

   _____

The effects of smoking on the heart and lungs

Diseases of the lungs

Lung cancer

Approximately 90 per cent of lung cancer victims smoke. Tar and other substances found in cigarettes cause cancer cells to form in the lungs. Non-smokers (passive smokers) who spend a lot of time in the company of smokers are also at risk.

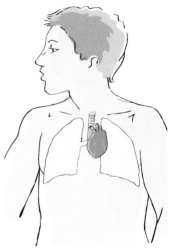

Bronchitis

Continuous smoking causes the tubes and the air sacs of the lungs to become filled with mucus or phlegm. The person tries to get rid of the phlegm by coughing it up; this is the 'smoker's cough'. Eventually the tubes and the air sacs become infected and the person goes down with bronchitis. The symptoms of bronchitis are fever, severe coughing and a feeling of not being able to get your breath. Permanent damage occurs when the air sacs become so choked that they become destroyed, leaving the person with permanent breathing difficulties. Bronchitis is the most common disease among smokers.

Emphysema

Emphysema is a very serious, incurable disease of the lungs. Smoking causes the lungs to become so badly damaged that they cannot function any more. Someone with emphysema would have trouble climbing stairs or doing anything else that requires energy. Seventy-five per cent of deaths from emphysema are smoking-related.

Diseases of the heart

Heart attacks

Smoking causes the hormone adrenaline to be released into the bloodstream. Adrenaline causes the heart to beat faster; over the years this puts strain on the heart. Eventually this could lead to a heart attack.

Arteriosclerosis

Smoking is one of the causes of arteriosclerosis or hardening of the arteries. This causes bad circulation which again puts strain on the heart and so increases the risk of heart failure.

Blood clots

Smoking also causes the blood to clot more easily in the blood vessels.

Passive smokers

Passive smokers, that is people who are frequently exposed to other people's smoke, in time run the same risks as actual smokers.

The effects of smoking on the rest of the body

- Strokes are usually caused when a blood clot forms in the brain. Strokes are more common in smokers than non-smokers. Strokes can give a person brain damage and leave them paralysed or partially paralysed. Strokes are a very common cause of disability in this country.
- The skin is affected by smoking; smokers tend to get more wrinkles and age more quickly than non-smokers.
- Smoking discolours teeth and hair.
- Smoking reduces your sense of taste and smell.

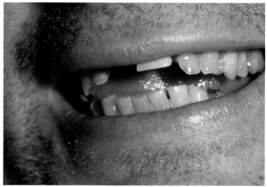

Smoking causes premature ageing and discoloration of hair and teeth

Smoking and pregnancy

If you smoke your baby smokes too.

- There is an increased risk of having a miscarriage or a stillborn baby.
- Babies of smokers are on average up to half a pound lighter than babies of non-smokers, and are more likely to be premature.
- Smoking around a baby after he or she is born increases the risk of cot death. At least 63 per cent of babies who die from cot death had mothers who smoke. At least 64 per cent had fathers who smoked. (Sudden Infant Death Registrar 2002).

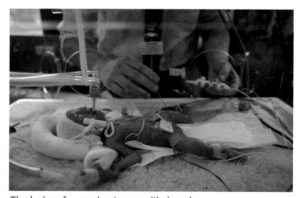

The baby of a smoker is more likely to be premature

- Smoking around a baby before or after he or she is born increases the risk of developing diseases such as bronchitis and asthma.
- Research shows delays in the physical, emotional and intellectual development of the babies of some smokers.
- Smoking reduces fertility in both men and women.
- Smoking causes menopause to come 1–2 years early.
- Smoking is linked to cancer of the womb and the cervix (opening of the womb).

What if I give up?

If a smoker decides to give up, the news is good.

- Some people who have been smoking for years believe that it is too late because the damage is done. This is not true – the risk of dying from smoking-related diseases reduces dramatically soon after the smoker quits.
- Women who stop smoking in the first 2–3 months of pregnancy are not at any greater risk of having low birth weight babies than women who did not smoke at all.
- Stopping smoking is a great achievement. It gives the smoker a sense of pride in having done something worthwhile.
- If you smoke a packet a day you can look forward to saving around €3,000 per year.
- Giving up improves the skin's appearance.
- Some people put on weight; about half a stone is usual. This weight will soon be lost again as people feel they have more energy and take more exercise.

⚙ ACTIVITY

Smoking quiz

1. What age do you have to be to legally buy cigarettes?_____

2. What is the major effect of smoking on the brain?
   _____

3. Describe in your own words what bronchitis is.
   _____
   _____

4. Describe in your own words what emphysema is.
   _____
   _____

5. What in your opinion is the worst effect of smoking during pregnancy?
   _____
   _____

6. What is passive smoking?
   _____
   _____

Cannabis

Origin

The drug cannabis, the world's most popular illegal drug, comes from a bushy plant called *Cannabis sativa*. Cannabis is grown in large quantities in South America, Africa, and Middle and Far Eastern countries such as Pakistan, Afghanistan, China, Cambodia, India and Iran. It is then smuggled from these countries to the rest of the world. Cannabis has been used as a drug for centuries, especially in China and Ancient Greece, where it was used as a medicine. Cannabis became very popular in America and Europe in the 1960s; in the 1980s its popularity declined, but it became fashionable again in the 1990s.

Cannabis takes three forms:

Cannabis herb is the leaves and flowers of the plant. It is also called marijuana, grass, dope, pot, weed, etc.

Cannabis resin is made when the plant is mixed with oil or resin and compressed or squashed into blocks. This substance is called hash, hashish, blow, etc.

Cannabis oil is produced when the juices are taken out of the plant and distilled to make them concentrated. This form is rare in Ireland.

What are the effects of cannabis use?

Short-term effects

- relaxation
- talkativeness
- giddiness
- feeling of slowed time
- sometimes colour, sensory and musical perception become altered.

Sometimes the short-term effects may not be pleasant. Here are some common ones:

vomiting	confusion	lack of co-ordination
headaches	fearfulness	panic attacks
paranoia		

Cannabis impairs your ability to ride a bicycle, drive a car or do anything else that requires good co-ordination.

Long-term effects

Some people believe that cannabis should be made legal, and that it doesn't really damage the user's health. Others believe that cannabis is a very harmful drug and that it definitely should not be made legal.

Facts about cannabis

- Cannabis contains 421 different chemicals. The most important and dangerous of these chemicals is THC. THC affects the brain, reproductive systems, lungs and the immune systems of heavy cannabis users. THC clings to the fatty tissue in your body and can be detected in the urine up to a month after taking a single joint.
- Cannabis has three times more cancer-causing tar than strong cigarettes.
- Cannabis smoking over prolonged periods can cause the following:
  – lack of interest/ambition
  – short-term memory loss
  – reduced learning ability
  – being absent a lot from school or work
  – dropping out of school.
- The male sex hormone testosterone reduces by 25–30 per cent within three hours of smoking cannabis.
- Women who smoke cannabis during pregnancy are likely to have:
  – a smaller baby
  – a baby who has less well-defined muscles
  – a baby who is more jittery, irritable and less attentive.
- Long-term cannabis use can trigger mental illness such as depression and schizophrenia.
- There is nothing in cannabis itself that causes people to try other illegal drugs. Even so, some research shows that cannabis users are more likely to experiment with other drugs than non-cannabis users.
- Cannabis use is illegal and if you are caught using or supplying cannabis a fine or imprisonment will result. A conviction for use or possession may damage your career prospects or hinder your ability to travel abroad.

 **ACTIVITY**

Test yourself on the questions below.

Question 1   Circle T (true) or F (false)

A.	Cannabis makes you more alert and better able to carry out tasks.	T	F
B.	Cannabis produces less tar than strong cigarettes.	T	F
C.	Cannabis is illegal.	T	F
D.	Cannabis is a newly discovered drug.	T	F
E.	Cannabis has a bad effect on the male and female reproductive systems.	T	F
F.	Cannabis traces stay in the body for a number of weeks.	T	F
G.	Cannabis helps you concentrate and do better at school/work.	T	F
H.	The most dangerous chemical in cannabis is called THC.	T	F
I.	Cannabis users are more likely to start using other drugs than non-cannabis users.	T	F
J.	If you are caught with cannabis you will be fined or imprisoned.	T	F

Question 2

Name three unpleasant short-term effects of cannabis use.

1. _____
2. _____
3. _____

Question 3

What do you consider to be the three most worrying long-term effects of cannabis use?

1. _____
2. _____
3. _____

Question 4

Why do you think cannabis users are more likely to use other illegal drugs?

_____
_____

ACTIVITY

Distribute the questionnaire below to other groups in your school or centre. Present your results using graphs, etc.

CANNABIS QUESTIONNAIRE

1. Age:

12-15 ☐
16-18 ☐
19 and over ☐

2. Are you: Male ☐   Female ☐

3. Please give your opinion on the following statements:

	Agree	Don't know	Disagree
A. Cannabis is a harmless drug	☐	☐	☐
B. Cannabis should be made legal	☐	☐	☐
C. Regular cannabis smoking can make a person less ambitious or interested in life.	☐	☐	☐
D. Cannabis use helps you concentrate.	☐	☐	☐
E. Cannabis smoking causes cancer.	☐	☐	☐

4. Have you ever smoked cannabis?   Yes ☐   No ☐

5. Do you know anyone who uses cannabis regularly?

Yes ☐   No ☐

6. Would you smoke cannabis if it were offered to you?

Yes ☐   No ☐

LSD

Origin

LSD was first manufactured in the 1920s although it did not come into common use until the 1960s and early 1970s during the 'hippie' era. LSD made a comeback at the end of the 1980s and the beginning of the 1990s. Acid house music gets part of its name from LSD's full name, which is lysergic acid diethylamide.

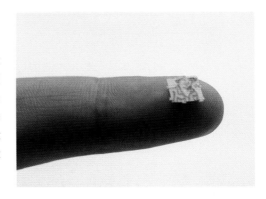

Appearance

LSD usually comes on strong paper sheets which have been dipped in the drug. Each sheet is made up of many small squares, which are torn off individually. Each square carries a logo. Common logos are bat wings, a black star, strawberries, mushrooms, a smiley face, etc.

Effects

LSD is a hallucinogenic drug which causes the user to hallucinate or become removed from reality. Sometimes hallucinations can be bad or frightening. When this happens it is called a 'bad trip'. Perhaps the most worrying effect of LSD use is that some users report having unpleasant flashbacks long after taking the drug.

ACTIVITY

Read the letter below and give your opinions in the space provided.

Dear Joan,

My name is Michael and I am 17 years old. Last weekend I went to a nightclub near where I live. I don't go out much so when I arrived and a few of the guys in my class came over I was really relieved. At least I wouldn't be standing there on my own all night. They seemed really delighted to see me. After talking to them for a while I realised they were definitely on something. I was praying they wouldn't ask me to take any, but of course they did. I didn't know what to do.

1. What pressures are there on Michael to take LSD?

_____

_____

2. If Michael takes the drug what could the consequences be?

_____

_____

3. If Michael refuses the drug what could the consequences be?

_____

_____

4. What would you do or say if you were in Michael's position?

_____

The truth about Ecstasy

Origin

Ecstasy is a drug that was invented in Germany before the First World War as a slimming aid: it causes the user to become energised and therefore burn up calories. The drug was never made legal, however, because it was not safe enough. Ecstasy was largely forgotten about until the 1980s and 1990s when 'house music' and 'rave' culture first became popular.

Appearance

Ecstasy or 'E' is sold under many different names; examples include 'doves' and 'shamrocks', reflected in the logo imprinted on them. Tablets are generally about the size of a paracetamol tablet. There are no official figures for Ecstasy use but it is thought that as many young people try Ecstasy as tobacco.

Short-term effects

- Blood pressure rises, the heart beats faster and the user's body temperature increases.
- The user feels relaxed and becomes friendly towards others.
- The user becomes full of energy.
- The user sweats a lot and feels thirsty.

Long-term effects

Because Ecstasy has only been popular since the 1980s, unfortunately not much is known about its long-term effects. It is thought, though, that the brain can suffer permanent damage in some cases.

Dangers!

Most people are aware that there have been a number of cases of young people dying from Ecstasy use. Dehydration is one of the main problems associated with the drug. Some nightclub owners have made money out of this problem, by turning taps off in the toilets and forcing dancers to buy water at inflated prices. Young people have suffered heart attacks, kidney failure, liver damage and heatstroke as a result of taking Ecstasy. There have been reports of others falling to their deaths because their co-ordination has been so badly impaired. Some young people have reported panic attacks and depression in the days and weeks following Ecstasy use.

 **CD - Track 4**

Listen to Track 4 and answer the questions.

1. How many people have died from Ecstasy use this year? _____

2. What did the post-mortem results reveal in this case?

    _____

    _____

3. How do the media normally portray or show drug users?

    _____

    _____

    _____

4. What information is there in this report to show that Ecstasy use spans all social and economic groups?

    _____

    _____

    _____

5. What does this report suggest should be done to help the problem?

    _____

    _____

Heroin

Origin

Heroin, like morphine, comes from the opium poppy. Pakistan and the Far East are the biggest heroin producers in the world. Heroin was used as a medicine until about three hundred years ago, when its effect on the mind became known. Heroin began to be used for non-medicinal purposes in the 1800s with the invention of the syringe.

Appearance

Heroin is sold as a white or brown powder in small packets or 'deals'. Heroin sold on the street is generally diluted or 'cut'. Sometimes dealers cut heroin with substances such as talcum powder, Vim or chalk dust, which makes it very dangerous to use. Heroin is injected, smoked or snorted and is sometimes called smack, junk or horse.

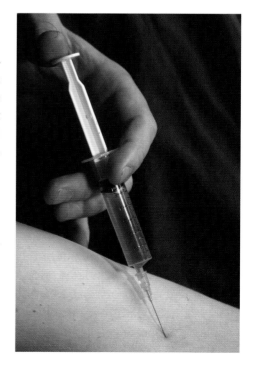

Effects of heroin use

The most widely publicised effect of heroin addiction is getting HIV and other viruses from the use of infected or 'dirty' needles. Even if a heroin addict does not contract HIV, their health frequently suffers. Heart failure, pneumonia, loss of appetite, weight loss and lung infections are common among users. Addicts sometimes overdose or unknowingly use heroin that is impure. This can result in death.

It is estimated that there are over 15,000 heroin addicts in Ireland. Unlike other drugs, which are equally popular across all the social classes, heroin use tends to be concentrated in areas of high unemployment and poverty. Ironically, heroin is one of the most expensive drugs available. It can cost over €125 per day to feed a habit. As a result some addicts resort to dealing or other crimes such as robbery to pay for their supply.

Withdrawing from heroin addiction can be very difficult. The addict may suffer bouts of diarrhoea, vomiting, headaches and the shakes. One minute the addict may feel boiling hot and the next freezing cold, and they may also hallucinate. These withdrawal symptoms are called 'cold turkey'.

ACTIVITY

Answer the following questions on heroin.

1. What do you think are the three most worrying effects of heroin addiction?

   _____

   _____

   _____

2. What effect does heroin abuse have on society in general?

   _____

   _____

3. Find out what a needle-exchange programme is. What is your opinion of this kind of programme?

   _____

   _____

Perhaps your class could watch a film that looks at the drugs issue. *Trainspotting* is a hard-hitting film about heroin addiction.

Cocaine

Cocaine, Ecstasy and amphetamines (e.g. Ritalin) are the most widely used illegal stimulant drugs in Ireland. (Ritalin is legal if it is prescribed by a doctor.)

Cocaine comes from the bushy coca plant, which is grown mainly in Colombia, Brazil and Bolivia. It is processed into a white powder known as 'coke', 'snow', 'Charlie' or 'blow'. For thousands of years South American people chewed coca leaves – in fact cocaine was an ingredient in Coca-Cola until 1888. However, the cocaine available on the street today is much more concentrated, highly addictive and very dangerous.

Cocaine users either inhale (snort) or inject the drug, which allows it to pass directly into the bloodstream thus causing an immediate high lasting 10–30 minutes.

Crack cocaine is produced when cocaine is chemically treated so that it forms a solid lump that can be smoked. Crack cocaine gets its name from the cracking sound that it makes when it's smoked.

Both cocaine and crack cocaine cause the brain to release large amounts of a natural brain chemical called dopamine. It is this flood of dopamine that causes the user to feel euphoric, energetic, as if they can do anything. Some users, however, may feel nervous or paranoid, and aggressive behaviour is common with crack cocaine use. When the drug wears off all users will feel depressed as their dopamine levels lower. With prolonged use the brain will stop producing dopamine on its own and so the user will need cocaine just to feel normal. This is why cocaine, especially crack cocaine, is so highly addictive.

Risks of cocaine use

- High blood pressure – risk of heart attacks and strokes.
- Sometimes the septum between the nostrils can become infected or even worn away as a result of snorting cocaine.
- Psychological problems, e.g. depression, paranoia, anxiety, mania, psychotic behaviour, schizophrenia-like behaviours.
- Infectious diseases, e.g. HIV, from sharing needles used to inject cocaine.
- Liver damage.
- Pregnant women who use cocaine are much more likely to have babies with serious birth defects or at the very least babies who are born premature and have a low birth weight.

Crack cocaine is often considered more dangerous than powder cocaine. It is cheaper and research shows that users are more likely to become aggressive or suicidal. It is also believed to be more addictive. Crack enters the bloodstream very quickly (8–10 seconds) but the high only lasts a few minutes. This means the addict has to quickly find more of the drug. Crack cocaine is believed to be behind much of the gun crime in the USA.

Using cocaine with other drugs

Using cocaine with other drugs, particularly alcohol, is even more dangerous. Cocaine and alcohol mix in the body to form another drug called cocaethylene, which can be lethal. Cocaethylene can cause the blood to thicken, thus raising blood pressure to very high levels and causing heart failure or damage. Many of the recent cocaine-related deaths have been linked to cocaethylene.

Facts about solvent abuse

Solvent abuse is the term given to the deliberate inhaling of gases or fumes from a number of commonly available substances. The main substances sniffed are:

- glue
- aerosols
- dry cleaning products
- paint thinner
- fuels, gas, petrol.

Effects:

- In Ireland up to ten people die from solvent abuse every year.
- Someone who has inhaled solvents appears to be drunk; they have slurred speech and stagger. Sometimes solvent abuse causes hallucinations.
- The next day the solvent abuser may have headaches, find it difficult to concentrate, have no appetite and suffer mood swings.
- If someone abuses solvents on a regular basis, there is usually weight loss, disturbed sleep and a characteristic rash around the user's mouth and nose.

 **ACTIVITY**

Eoin's story

Eoin started on solvents when he was about 14 years old. Every evening he and a few friends would go up onto some waste ground near where they lived to sniff whatever substance they had been able to get their hands on that day. The hardware store in their area was getting very suspicious and was starting to refuse to give any sort of solvents to young people. Eoin knew how to get around this problem. All he had to do was to go to a shop in a 'posh' area about two miles away; he never had any trouble getting solvents there.

Eoin knew that his solvent habit was having a bad effect on him, but nobody else seemed worried. His parents were too busy fighting to notice any change in him. Most of his teachers didn't really notice him either. He wasn't particularly good at school so the fact that his results were getting worse didn't seem to trouble anyone.

Can you finish the story?

_____

_____

_____

_____

Help for people suffering from drug addiction

If you feel that you or someone you know is suffering from or at risk of suffering from drug addiction you should contact your GP, who will put you in contact with your local addiction service. In addition, the voluntary organisation Narcotics Anonymous (phone: 01 830 0944) is open 24 hours and may also be able to give advice.

Alcohol

Attitudes to and images of alcohol

Alcohol is one product that is heavily advertised on TV and in the print media. Advertisers use various techniques to convince you to buy their products. Here are some of them.

Use of a famous/glamorous/sexy person

This person will claim that he or she uses the product and finds it really good. The ad wants you to believe that if you use this product you will be sexy and glamorous too and have lots of friends.

Can you think of one alcohol advertisement that uses this technique?

_____

_____

Humour

Can you think of one alcohol advertisement that uses this technique?

_____

_____

Exaggeration

An example of this: 'the best built car in the world'.

Can you think of one alcohol advertisement that uses this technique?

_____

_____

Slogans

An example of this is 'Live life to the power of Guinness'.

Can you think of one other alcohol advertisement that uses this technique?

_____

_____

⚙ ACTIVITY

Look at the alcohol advertisement pictured here. Answer the following questions:

1. What is the name of the alcoholic drink being advertised here?

   _____

2. What advertising technique is being used?

   _____

3. Who do you think this ad is aimed at?

   _____

   Give a reason for your answer.

   _____

   _____

4. What is this ad implying? If you drink this product you will . . .

   _____

   _____

Addictions

When someone becomes physically, socially or psychologically dependent on a substance or a behaviour they are said to be addicted to or dependent on that substance or behaviour.

 **ACTIVITY**

> Can you think of five common substances or behaviours that people can become addicted to?
>
> 1. _____
> 2. _____
> 3. _____
> 4. _____
> 5. _____

Alcohol misuse or addiction

In the past people were called alcoholics if they frequently drank in excessive quantities. This term brought with it images of people down and out, begging for their next drink. In more recent times the word 'alcoholic' has been replaced by 'problem drinker' or 'alcohol misuser'. This has been in an effort to make people realise that you do not have to be on the streets, drinking a bottle of cheap cider, to be a problem drinker. In fact there is evidence to show that the highest level of problem drinking occurs among doctors and dentists.

The effects of alcohol misuse on the body

The liver

Alcohol is poisonous to the body. The liver is the organ which breaks alcohol down into substances that do not harm the body. It can safely break down about one unit of alcohol per hour. If a person frequently drinks heavily, the liver cannot cope and becomes damaged. Cirrhosis of the liver is the disease that results. This disease can be fatal. Other diseases such as gout, where there is a painful swelling of the joints, usually of the toes, are common in heavy drinkers.

The stomach

Alcohol irritates the stomach and can cause ulcers, which are sores on the lining of the stomach.

The brain

Long-term misuse of alcohol can cause brain damage. If you have a blackout, brain cells are being killed that are not being replaced. If this occurs frequently, the person can become permanently brain-damaged, for example with their memory badly affected.

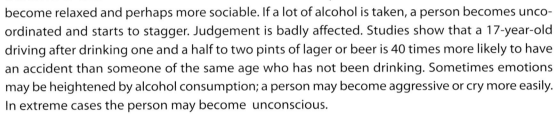

Other effects on the individual

If alcohol is taken in moderate amounts it causes the person to become relaxed and perhaps more sociable. If a lot of alcohol is taken, a person becomes unco-ordinated and starts to stagger. Judgement is badly affected. Studies show that a 17-year-old driving after drinking one and a half to two pints of lager or beer is 40 times more likely to have an accident than someone of the same age who has not been drinking. Sometimes emotions may be heightened by alcohol consumption; a person may become aggressive or cry more easily. In extreme cases the person may become unconscious.

Effects of parental alcohol misuse

Given that approximately one in ten Irish people are problem drinkers or alcohol misusers, there must be large numbers of Irish families affected by the problem. Children who grow up in a family where there is a problem drinker have a lot to cope with. The problem drinker can be very inconsistent: one minute the loving parent, the next a selfish drinker who doesn't seem to care how much hurt he or she causes. Sometimes the problem drinker can get violent or verbally abusive when drunk. This makes living with the person very stressful.

Studies of homes affected by alcohol misuse show that children in these families frequently take on one of four different personalities or roles in an effort to cope with living in a stressful environment. The four roles or personalities are as follows:

- Hero
- Scapegoat
- Lost child
- Mascot.

Hero

This child works hard, is very mature and responsible. He or she tries to hold the family together and solve the family's problems. The hero wants to show the outside world that their family is a good, respectable one.

Scapegoat

This child appears to be the opposite of the hero. He or she gets into trouble in school and acts irresponsibly. When this child becomes a teenager, she or he is likely to break other rules, e.g. under-age drinking, drug use, sex from an early age. There is a high instance of unexpected teenage pregnancy among these children. The reason for the scapegoat's behaviour is to take attention away from the drinking parent. Everyone will be giving out and worried about the scapegoat, not the drinker.

Lost child

This child is quiet and very undemanding. He or she asks for nothing. This child sees all the trouble the drinker and the scapegoat are causing and thinks that if she or he is practically invisible this will help the family's problems go away.

Mascot

The mascot is usually the youngest child in the family. He or she is treated like a baby by the rest of the family and told that there is nothing wrong. This child becomes very confused as a result.

When these children become adults, they do not suddenly drop these roles.
Without help:

- The hero stays much as he or she is, and frequently marries someone who has a drink problem whom they can look after.
- The scapegoat is vulnerable to addiction.
- The lost child finds it hard to form close relationships.
- The mascot tries to remain a child and has trouble being responsible.

 **CD - Track 5**

Listen to Jackie giving an account of her family on Track 5. Can you identify who is in each role?

Who is the hero? _____

Who is the scapegoat? _____

Who is the lost child? _____

Who is the mascot? _____

Alcohol and the law

 **ACTIVITY**

Read the information and answer the questions that follow.

Because alcohol can be a dangerous drug, its use has always been controlled by society. Licensing laws state when, where and to whom alcohol can be sold. Other legal controls on the use of alcohol relate to drunkenness, drink driving and age restrictions on the sale of alcoholic drinks to young people.

Licensing laws

- Pubs, restaurants, hotels, sports and social clubs, if they are to allow people to buy and drink alcohol on the premises, must have a drinks licence. Drinks licences are granted by the courts.
- Off-licences have a licence to sell alcohol, but people cannot drink it on the premises. Off-licences must close at 10 p.m.
- Pubs are allowed to open between 10.30 a.m. and 11.30 p.m. (12 p.m. summer) Monday–Wednesday. Thursday–Saturday opening times are 10.30 a.m.–12.30 a.m. unless the pub has an 'extension'. On a Sunday pubs may open all day from 12.30 p.m.–11.00 p.m. (11.30 p.m. summer). Pubs must also close on Christmas Day and on Good Friday. Half an hour's drink-up time is allowed every day.
- It is permissible to brew beer and wine at home but not spirits such as poteen.

Age restrictions

- It is an offence to give alcohol to a child under five years of age, and children under 15 years are only allowed into a pub during permitted hours if they are accompanied by a parent or guardian.
- It is an offence to sell alcohol to a person under 18 years of age in either a pub or an off-licence. The pub or off-licence owner can be fined for doing so and their drinks licence endorsed.
- If you are under 18 it is against the law for you to buy or consume alcohol in a public place. If you do so, you may face a fine.
- If a garda suspects with 'reasonable cause' that you are under 18 and have bought or are consuming alcohol in a public place, you are obliged to give your correct name, age and address. If you give false details, you may face a fine. The garda can also confiscate the alcohol.
- You cannot work as a bar person if you are under the age of 18.

Drinking and driving

It is an offence to drive under the influence of alcohol. If you have more than 80mg of alcohol per 100ml of blood, you are deemed to be under the influence. This limit can be exceeded by some people if they drink only one pint of beer. (At the time of going to press a limit of 50mg alcohol per 100ml of blood had been proposed.)

1. What age do you have to be to work in a pub? _____
2. What is the law in relation to home brewing?

   _____

3. At what time can pubs open in the morning? _____
4. What is the legal winter closing time on a Tuesday?

   _____

5. What is the legal summer closing time on a Saturday?

   _____

6. What age must you be to buy alcohol? _____
7. What is the law in relation to drinking and driving?

   _____

   _____

8. When can a garda take alcohol from a young person?

   _____

   _____

9. Do you think there is a need for laws relating to alcohol?

   Yes ▢   No ▢

   Give a reason for your answer.

   _____

   _____

10. At what time must off-licences close by law? _____

ACTIVITY

Investigate how smoking, alcohol and other drugs are portrayed in magazines and other print media. Present a collage of your findings.

ACTIVITY

Ask other groups in your school/centre to fill out this or a similar questionnaire. Present your results using bar charts, etc. Be sure to point out that there are no names on the questionnaires and that answers will be treated in confidence.

ALCOHOL QUESTIONNAIRE

Are you: Male ☐   Female ☐

Age group: 12–15 ☐
                     16–18 ☐
          19 and over ☐

1. Do you drink alcohol?   Yes ☐   No ☐

2. If yes, how often? (Please tick)
    Once a week ☐
    More than once a week ☐
    Less than once a week ☐

3. On average how much would you drink on a night out?
    1–4 drinks or units ☐
    5–8 drinks or units ☐
    More than 8 drinks or units ☐

Note: 1 drink = 1/2 pint of beer, lager or cider, 1 shot of spirits or 1 glass of wine.

4. Have you ever been drunk?   Yes ☐   No ☐

5. Have you ever been sick as a result of drinking?
                              Yes ☐   No ☐

6. Have you ever forgotten parts of the night?
                              Yes ☐   No ☐

7. Attitudes to alcohol (Please tick)   Agree   Disagree

• Almost everybody drinks.   ☐

• You don't need to drink to have a good night.   ☐   ☐

• People who don't drink are generally 'dry'.   ☐   ☐

• Very few people develop problems with drink.   ☐   ☐

• Alcohol is responsible for many family problems.   ☐   ☐

KEY ASSIGNMENT

For this key assignment you must collect information on healthy lifestyles. One of the best places to get this is the HSE health promotion website (ww.healthpromotion.ie). This website allows you to download or order a huge range of health promotion materials and leaflets on a wide variety of topics. (This activity will fulfil the second part of Key Assignment 2.)

When you have completed this key assignment, go to page 1 and tick off Assignment 2 on the checklist.

🔍 KEY ASSIGNMENT

For this key assignment you must present a report on a drug that you have studied as part of this Social Education module. You can get information for your report from this book, and another good source of information is the HSE-funded website www.drugs.ie.

Your report should include the following:

- Name of the drug, including any slang names.
- Where the drug comes from.
- How the drug is taken, e.g. smoked, injected.
- What are the main risks associated with taking the drug?

📄 EXAM TIME

Social Education (2005) – short questions

1. Which of the following is a hallucinogenic drug?

Social Education (2005) – long question (part)

2. The World Health Organisation defines health as:

> A complete state of physical, mental and social well-being and not simply the absence of disease or infirmity.

Why is the above definition of health a good one?

_____

_____

Social Education (2005) – long question

3. # Youth Health Time Bomb

Many teenagers are knocking years off their lifespan as they increasingly turn to drink, drugs, sex and cigarettes. Even with the greatest advances in medical science doctors will be unable to reverse the levels of disease in the future. Children as young as 11 are now experimenting with binge drinking.

Experts are expecting a time bomb of lifestyle-related diseases to emerge in years to come. Part of the problem is that that most young people believe that it will never happen to them and if it does they imagine it is too far into the future to worry about.

Already health professionals are treating lung cancer in people in their thirties, and sexually transmitted diseases in an increasing number of teenagers. Because the damage takes some time to become evident many young people are not worried about tomorrow's problems.

The latest statistics show that 25 per cent of males and 30 per cent of females in the 17–18 age bracket are now smoking. This is frightening, as people will have lost half their lung function before they start feeling breathless. For unluckier smokers, cancer will catch them first. Amazingly the reason many give for not quitting is concern about weight gain. Yet many know that smoking is a major factor in premature ageing.

The culture of binge drinking in Ireland will lead to cardiovascular and organ problems in the future. Excessive alcohol consumption can lead to killer diseases, premature ageing, violence and depression. Socially, alcohol abuse leads to many problems and chief among them is the increased numbers engaged in unprotected casual sex. Experts say poor lifestyle choices made as a teenager will have huge consequences for later life.

The way we live today is the way we will look and feel in the future. It is not always today or tomorrow that our lifestyle choices will affect us but when they do impact on us their effects will be mainly irreversible and probably fatal.

(a) Are there more teenage males or more teenage females smoking? Use evidence from the article to support your answer.

_____

_____

(b) Based on the information in the article, list three different diseases that these young people might face in the future. In the case of each explain the cause.

Disease: _____

Cause: _____

Disease: _____

Cause: _____

Disease: _____

Cause: _____

(c) Outline **three** pieces of advice, other than the issues raised in the article, you would give to teenagers to help them make positive lifestyle choices.

1. _____

2. _____

3. _____

Social Education (2006) – long question (part)

4.

Golden tan	**Glossy hair**
Perfect pecs	**Bleached teeth**
Clear skin	**Six pack**
Ultra slim	

(a) Explain how the body image as presented by the media might lead to health problems for young people.

1. _____

2. _____

(b) The strategic task force on alcohol recommends 'A ban on all alcohol advertising and sponsorship wherever children may be exposed to it and a total ban on television advertising'.

Do you think this recommendation would help tackle the problem of teenage drinking in Ireland? Explain your answer.

_____

_____

_____

Social Education (2007) – short questions

5. The recommended daily intake of water is:

Eight litres   Eight pints   Eight glasses

6. The fertility of a male who smokes cannabis regularly is:

Reduced   Increased   Unchanged

7. How many units of alcohol are contained in a pint of lager?

1 Unit   1.5 Units   2 Units

Social Education (2007) – long question (part)

A balanced diet

8. (a) Select one of the requirements for 'a balanced diet' listed above. Name one example/source of this requirement.

Requirement: _____

Example: _____

(b) State why the requirement mentioned in (a) is important for a healthy body.

_____

_____

9.

Drink Culture – A Worrying Trend

Irish teenagers rank among the worst binge drinkers in Europe according to recent study of schools in 35 countries.

Excessive drinking can lead to many health problems. Other than physical health problems describe **two** other possible problems facing Irish teenagers who binge drink.

1. _____

2. _____

Social Education (2008) – short questions

10. Fish, meat and poultry are all important sources of:

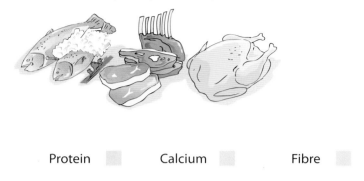

Protein ▢   Calcium ▢   Fibre ▢

Social Education (2008) – long question (part)

11.

Time to shatter myth about glamour drug

There is a need to shatter the myth that cocaine is a glamour drug used by the wealthy. There is an increase in the demand for this drug and an increase in the numbers of cocaine users. These users come from all social and economic backgrounds. Many naively believe that they have no connection to gangland wars and criminality but their use of the drug is unwittingly helping to fund the trade and is keeping the drug lords in business.

Some see cocaine as a party drug, a fun thing, a cool thing. This acceptance of cocaine makes getting to grips with the problem even harder. The perception of cocaine as a safe drug needs to be addressed given the levels of risk behaviours associated with using this drug. The impact of cocaine use on the community and on families should not be underestimated.

Individuals are experiencing relationship breakdown, problems at work, loss of employment, as well as crippling debt.

Health problems caused by cocaine use include damage to the heart, lungs, brain, kidneys and nose. Injecting cocaine is associated with a rise in HIV infections, abscesses, amputations and even death.

The government's response to the cocaine problem has been too slow and the drug barons are winning the battle. Services however are now gearing up to deal with cocaine importation and use.

Dorothy Madden

Daily Times

(a) How are those who buy drugs unwittingly helping the drug trade?

_____

_____

(b) Explain how cocaine use can affect individuals and communities.

Individuals: _____

_____

Communities: _____

_____

_____

(c) Describe two things that the government is doing to combat the problem of cocaine importation and use in Ireland.

1. _____

2. _____

12.

(a) Why are government warnings on cigarette packets a good idea?

_____

(b) State **two** laws/regulations governing smoking in Ireland.

1. _____

2. _____

UNIT 3 Relationships and Sexuality

Sex Role or Gender Stereotyping

Sex role or gender stereotyping is when we have a fixed and over-simplified idea of what it means to be male or female. People who stereotype others according to their gender often have incorrect ideas about men and women's personalities, abilities and life expectations.

Read the gender-stereotyped jokes below. How are men and women's (a) personalities, (b) abilities and (c) life expectations stereotyped in them?

(*Note*: The following 'jokes' are not meant to offend. They are merely being used here to illustrate our society's stereotypical views.)

Men

- Few women admit their age; few men act it.
- Go for younger men. You might as well – they never mature anyway.
- What's the difference between men and women? A woman wants one man to satisfy her every need whereas a man wants every woman to satisfy his one need.
- How do you scare a man? Sneak up behind him and start throwing confetti.
- There are a lot of words you could use to describe men – sensitive, caring, loving – they'd be wrong but you could still use them.
- How do you keep a man from reading your emails? Rename the folder 'instruction manuals'.
- The children of Israel wandered around the desert for forty years. Even in biblical times, men wouldn't ask for directions.
- Only a man would buy a €1,000 car and put a €2,000 stereo in it.

Women

- Why do women have smaller feet than men? So they can stand closer to the cooker.
- Why do brides wear white? So that the dishwasher will match the oven and the fridge.
- If your dog is barking at the back door and your wife is yelling at the front door, who do you let in first? The dog of course . . . at least he'll shut up after you let him in.
- I haven't spoken to my wife for 18 months – I don't like to interrupt her.
- What type of books do women like? Cheque books.

Women in the workforce

You can get a good indication of how society currently views male and female roles by looking at workforce trends.

Look at some of the labour statistics from the 2006 census and answer the questions that follow.

Occupation	Males	Females
Accountants	15,373	11,743
Army	7,042	400
Barristers and solicitors	5,328	4,675
Bank/building society managers	4,883	3,741
Bus drivers	6,891	783
Bus inspectors	432	28
Butchers	5,423	257
Care attendants	3,456	30,255
Carpenters	37,586	183
Chefs	12,327	9,639
Child care workers	495	16,847
Classroom assistants	408	9,104
Cleaners	7,115	22,527
Computer engineers	3,007	426
Dentists	1,039	676
Doctors	6,124	3,981
Electricians	25,437	289
Farmers	80,117	8,297
Fire fighters	1,794	62
Flight attendants	930	2,739
Forklift drivers	10,914	117
Gardaí	10,026	2,299
Judges	140	57
Mechanics	13,878	148
Nurses	3,957	47,188
Painters and decorators	12,291	361
Plumbers	15,885	80
Prison officers	2,187	350

Secretaries	652	30,226
Security guards	11,690	1,132
Sewing machinists	442	2,260
Social workers	4,761	12,933
Taxi drivers	34,554	557
Teachers	23,379	57,519
Truck drivers	34,554	557
Vets	1,270	415
Waiters and waitresses	2,770	12,525

Questions

1. Name the three occupations from the above list that you think command the biggest wages.

   (a) _____

   (b) _____

   (c) _____

   Are these occupations male- or female-dominated? Support your answer with information from the table.

   _____

   _____

   _____   _____

2. Name the three occupations from the above list that you think command the lowest wages.

   (a) _____

   (b) _____

   (c) _____

   Are these occupations male- or female-dominated? Support your answer with information from the table.

   _____

   _____

   _____

3. What percentage of bus drivers are male? _____

4. What percentage of army personnel are female? _____

CD - Track 6

On Track 6 you will hear a group of students and their teacher having a discussion about sex-role and gender stereotyping. The discussion is divided into two parts. Listen carefully and answer the questions that follow.

Part 1

1. What definition of gender stereotyping did the class come up with?

   _____
   _____
   _____
   _____
   _____

2. List four examples from the discussion of how men and women's personalities are sometimes sex-role or gender stereotyped by society.

   Men
   A. _____
   B. _____
   C. _____
   D. _____
   Women
   A. _____
   B. _____
   C. _____
   D. _____

Part 2

3. What definition of gender-role stereotyping did the class come up with?

   _____
   _____
   _____

4. List four examples from the discussion of how men and women's roles are sex-role or gender stereotyped by society.

   Men's roles
   A. _____
   B. _____
   C. _____

D. _____

Women's roles

A. _____

B. _____

C. _____

D. _____

5. List four suggestions the class made about how ideas about sex-role or gender-stereotyping are formed.

A _____

B. _____

C. _____

D. _____

🔍 KEY ASSIGNMENT

For this key assignment you need to form a small group of three or four people. As a group collect pictures and information from magazines, newspapers and the Internet and use them to make a collage illustrating ways in which the media promote sex-role stereotyping. Advertisements will be particularly useful.

When you have completed this key assignment, go to page 1 and tick off Assignment 3 on the checklist.

Relationships

Unlike some animals that are solitary, people are social beings. Getting on with others and forming relationships is important to all of us. Many of us worry about how we appear to others. We worry about not being liked or accepted. This can be particularly true for teenagers and young adults when they start to want to form sexual relationships.

The ability to form relationships, whether sexual or not, does not come naturally to everyone. It is not a skill that we are born with, but one that we develop and perfect over the years. This is why people who do not see or experience healthy relationships during their childhood can find it difficult to form stable, loving relationships later in life.

The male reproductive system

Label the diagram below:

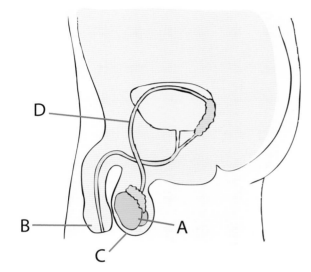

A _____

B _____

C _____

D _____

From puberty onwards, the male testes produce sperm. The testes are held outside the body in a sac called the scrotum. The testes also produce the male sex hormone testosterone, which is responsible for the production of sperm and causing changes at puberty such as the voice breaking, and the growth of pubic and facial hair.

When the male reaches orgasm during intercourse, sperm travels from the testes through tubes called the vas deferens to the penis where it is then released far up in the woman's vagina near the cervix. The sperm then swim frantically towards the woman's Fallopian tubes in an effort to fertilise the egg, which may or may not be there. In the end only one sperm fertilises the egg, even though many thousands are released.

Pregnancy and Birth

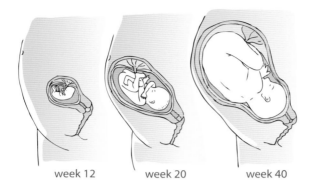

week 12   week 20   week 40

Match these words and definitions.

1. A male sex hormone _____
2. Vas deferens _____
3. Produce sperm _____
4. Where the egg is fertilised _____
5. Uterus _____
6. A female sex hormone _____
7. Cervix _____
8. Puberty _____
9. Conception _____
10. Ovulation _____

a. Transition into adulthood
b. Testosterone
c. Fertilisation
d. Womb
e. Releasing an egg every month
f. Fallopian tubes
g. Joins testes to the penis
h. Opening of the womb
i. Oestrogen
j. Testes

Answer the following questions on pregnancy in the spaces provided.

1. Name three functions of the placenta.

A. _____

B. _____

C. _____

2. Explain how women who drink, smoke or take other drugs while pregnant are putting their babies at risk.

_____

_____

3. What is an episiotomy? _____

4. Give two reasons why a baby may be born by Caesarean section.

    A. _____

    B. _____

Work out the due date from the information given below.

Mary has just done a pregnancy test which has turned out positive. She now wants to calculate her expected due date.

The first day of her last period was 6 October.

When will the baby be due?

_____

Foetal Alcohol Syndrome

Foetal alcohol syndrome is the most common preventable cause of mental retardation in children. It is caused by a mother drinking alcohol during pregnancy. Because Ireland does not register births by specific disability it is not known how many babies are born every year here with FAS. Figures from other cultures with drinking habits similar to ours, however, estimate the figure to be as high as one in one hundred births. This figure does not seem to be too outlandish given that approximately one in ten Irish people are  problem drinkers. The symptoms of FAS are both physical and mental. Not all symptoms may be present.

Mental problems

- Developmental delays, e.g. delayed speech.
- Behavioural problems, e.g. extreme anger, poor attention span, hyperactivity.
- Emotional problems, e.g. low self-esteem.

- Learning problems: the average IQ of someone with FAS is 68 (normal IQ is 100) (Streissguth, 1991). Some children with FAS have IQs as low as 20, which means they are severely retarded.
- Difficulty with maths in particular.
- Newborns may have irregular sleep/awake cycles.
- Poor social skills.

These problems stay with the child throughout their lives, causing them untold hardship and pain.

Physical problems
- Miscarriage, stillbirth or death in the first few weeks of life.
- Developmental delays, e.g. delay in sitting up, crawling, walking.
- Smaller than average head.
- Short stature.
- Low birth weight.
- Poor muscle tone.
- Poor weight gain.
- Characteristic facial features – small eye openings, thin upper lip, small chin, small short nose, flat nasal bridge, flat philtrum (groove between nose and upper lip).
- Small finger- and toenails.
- Dental crowding with permanent teeth.
- Poor suck and seizures (newborns).
- Sometimes cleft palate, congenital heart defects, strabismus (squint), hearing loss, poor eyesight, defects of the spine and joints.
- Asymmetrical ears – one ear either higher or bigger than the other.

There is no safe limit for alcohol during pregnancy – so it is best not to drink at all. Studies show that even moderate drinking, i.e. two to four units per day (one to two pints) can cause FAS.

Foetal Alcohol Syndrome is a lifelong condition. Streissguth (1996), following up on 90 adolescents and adults with FAS, found that over 90 per cent of them had mental health problems, e.g. depression, panic attacks, psychosis, suicide attempts. Over 80 per cent were unemployed and the vast majority had severe drug and alcohol problems themselves. (See www.faslink.org/diagnose.htm.)

> **There is no treatment for Foetal Alcohol Syndrome – NEVER drink during pregnancy.**

Contraception

Information leaflets on contraception are available from health promotion units: there should be one close to you.

The pill

There are two types: the combined pill and progesterone only. The pill makes the body think it is already pregnant and if taken every day at the same time it is very reliable. It is available on prescription only.

Natural methods

By recording natural signs and symptoms, for example increases in temperature, couples can recognise the woman's fertile time. Couples avoid sex during this time. This is not a very reliable method and is usually used when religious beliefs do not permit the use of artificial methods.

Injectable contraceptives

An injection is given to the woman every 12 weeks. This works in the same way as the pill. It is a very safe method.

Coil

This is fitted into the womb by a doctor and stops the egg from implanting. It is a very safe method and is usually used after a woman has had children.

Condoms

There are both male and female condoms. Both stop sperm entering the vagina. They must be used very carefully to be effective.

Diaphragm, also known as a cap

This is inserted into the vagina before intercourse and blocks sperm from travelling up to the egg. It must be used with a spermicide cream (which kills sperm).

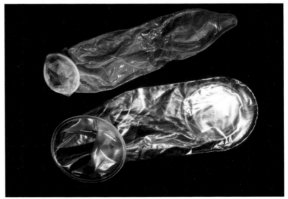

Male and female condoms

Note: using a male condom is the only method that helps prevent the spread of sexually transmitted infections.

HIV and Aids

Aids (Acquired Immunodeficiency Syndrome) has been described as the plague of the twentieth and twenty-first centuries. The disease Aids is the final, life-threatening illness caused by HIV (Human Immunodeficiency Virus). The first cases of Aids were identified in America in 1981, although researchers have evidence to show that the virus has been around in central Africa from as early as 1950.

At the end of 2007 it was estimated that there were about 30.8 million adults and 2.5 million children worldwide infected with the virus (World Health Organisation, 2007). In Ireland during 2006, 337 new cases were reported to the Health Protection Surveillance Centre in Dublin. In the first half of 2007 a total of 205 cases were reported, indicating that infection rates are rising in this country.

When HIV enters the body the person is said to be HIV positive. When the virus begins to destroy large numbers of T-cells, which are a type of white blood cell, the person is said to have developed Aids. White blood cells are used by the body to fight infection and disease, so without them we are prone to all sorts of illnesses and infections. It is one of these infections, most commonly pneumonia, that eventually kills the Aids sufferer. It may take as long as fifteen years for someone with HIV to develop full-blown Aids.

There are a number of ways in which HIV can be spread:

- Unprotected (male–female) sexual intercourse with an infected person (66%).
- Unprotected (male–male) sexual intercourse with an infected person (8%).
- Intravenous drug users sharing infected needles (10%).
- Infected mother to unborn child (11%). During 2007 115 babies were born to HIV-infected mothers in Ireland: 72 are not infected and 43 remain of indeterminate status (Health Protection Surveillance Centre, 2008).
- Through transfusions (5%). All blood is now tested in Ireland so this should no longer be a source of infection in this country.

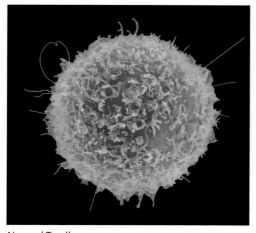

Normal T-cells

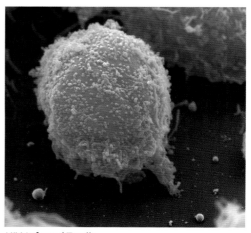

HIV-infected T-cells

Symptoms

Stage 1

No symptoms. During the first stages of HIV infection the symptoms do not show up. People can live with being HIV positive without even knowing it.

Stage 2

Mild illness. At this stage the virus grows within the white blood cells and destroys them. The white blood cells fight disease in our bodies and so when large numbers of them are destroyed, the body's defences weaken. The person may begin to feel frequently tired, lose weight or develop a cough, diarrhoea or fever and not be able to fight it.

Stage 3

Severe illness. By this time the virus has practically destroyed the body's immune system, so that it is not able to fight even the most common illnesses. Eventually the person picks up an illness that kills them. Pneumonia is a common one.

Treatment

Like all viral infections (viruses are so small that they can enter a human body cell – if you kill them you also kill the body cell) HIV/Aids are as yet incurable. Scientists working against HIV have come up with three different strategies.

- Drugs that will prevent HIV reproducing, e.g AZT.
- Drugs that will help block HIV from entering human body cells.
- Education programmes about the dangers of HIV, how it is spread and how it can be prevented.

ACTIVITY

Answer the questions below.

1. How is Aids different from HIV?

_____

_____

2. Explain the four main ways in which HIV is or has been transmitted.

_____

_____

3. Benny has been sharing needles with his friends to inject steroids. Explain why Benny's sexual partner, Michelle, may be at risk of getting the HIV infection.

_____
_____
_____

4. Many teenagers report that they do not use condoms when having sex. What are some of the reasons they might give for not using them?

_____
_____
_____

5. Explain why an HIV-infected person is much more likely to get a chest infection than a non-infected person.

_____
_____

6. What is the main drug used in the treatment of Aids patients?

_____

Living with Aids: Terry's story

I vividly recall a night in December or January about a year ago. It was six p.m., very cold and getting dark. I was waiting for a bus to go home, standing behind a tree for protection from the wind.

I had recently lost a friend to Aids. From whatever measure of intuition God had given me, I knew suddenly and quite certainly that I also had Aids. I stood behind the tree and cried. I was afraid. I was alone and I thought I had lost everything that was ever dear to me. In that place, it was very easy to imagine losing my home, my family, my friends, and my job. The possibility of dying under that tree, in the cold, utterly cut off from any human love, seemed very real. I prayed through my tears. Over and over, I prayed, 'Let this cup pass.' But I knew. Several months later, in April, the doctor told me what I had discovered for myself.

Now, it is nearly a year. I am still here, still working, still living, still learning how to love. There are some inconveniences. This morning, just out of curiosity, I counted the number of pills I have to take during the course of a week. It came to 112 assorted tablets and capsules. I go to the doctor once a month and find myself reassuring him that I feel quite well. He mutters to himself and re-reads the latest laboratory results which show my immune system declining to zero.

My last T-cell count was 10. A normal count is in the range of 800–1,600. I have been fighting painful sores in my mouth that make eating difficult. But, frankly, food has always been more important to me than a little pain. I have had thrush for a year. It never quite goes away. Recently, the doctor discovered the herpes virus had gotten hold of my system. There have been strange fungal infections. One was on my tongue. A biopsy caused my tongue to swell and I couldn't talk for a week, making many of my good friends secretly thankful. A way had been found to shut me up and they all revelled in the relative peace and quite. Of course, there are night sweats, fevers, swollen lymph glands, and unbelievable fatigue.

The head of the local health department in my area was quoted recently saying she believes there is a conspiracy of silence on Aids. She reports that of the 187 deaths in this area from Aids not one has listed Aids as the cause of death in an obituary.

It appears that this conspiracy of silence involves those who have Aids, or are infected with the virus, as well as the general public which still seems to have a difficult time discussing the subject.

ACTIVITY

1. When Terry was standing under the tree waiting for the bus he prayed for God to 'let this cup pass'. What do you think he meant by this?

   _____

   _____

2. What are T-cells and why is it serious for Terry to have such a low count?

   _____

   _____

3. What main health problems is Terry having?

   _____

   _____

4. Apart from Terry's health problems, what other problems do you think he might encounter in his everyday life?

   _____

   _____

5. Why do you think that out of the 187 deaths from Aids in the area of the United States where Terry lives, no one wanted to declare Aids publicly as the cause of death?

   _____

   _____

6. Imagine that you are Terry's partner. How do you think you would have felt and what do you think you would have done when Terry was first diagnosed as having Aids?

   _____

   _____

Other Sexually Transmitted Infections (STIs)

Sexually transmitted infections are caused by various bacteria, viruses and fungi. They are passed from an infected person to a non-infected person through sexual activity. Sexually transmitted infections can be avoided by avoiding high-risk behaviours. High-risk behaviours include having multiple, or many, different sex partners, having sex without the man wearing a condom (although wearing a condom does not guarantee safety), or having sex with people you do not know very well. A person may show no symptoms, yet still be infectious and contagious. Information on STIs in Ireland is available on the Health Protection Surveillance Centre (formerly the National Disease Surveillance Centre) website www.ndsc.ie. GPs and other health professionals must notify the HPSC of any STI cases presented to them – this is done anonymously.

STIs caused by bacteria

Syphilis

Figures for syphilis infection have risen dramatically over the past number of years. The annual average number of reported cases from 1989 to 1999 was 14. This annual average has now risen to 246 new cases each year.

Symptoms
The symptoms of syphilis occur in three stages:

Stage 1
Pimple-like sores appear in the infected area: they may disappear again.
Stage 2
A rash appears, especially on the hands and feet. There may also be fever, swollen lymph glands, sore throat, patchy hair loss, weight loss, headaches, muscle aches and tiredness.
Stage 3
Syphilis remains in the body and begins to attack the internal organs including the brain, nerves, eyes, heart, blood vessels, liver, lungs, bones and joints. Untreated syphilis causes paralysis, blindness, dementia and death.

If a pregnant woman has syphilis her unborn baby is in grave danger. The infection can cause stillbirths, neonatal death, deafness, brain damage and bone deformities. Sometimes babies are born with no symptoms, but develop them in the first weeks of life.

Treatment
Antibiotics, especially penicillium.

Gonorrhoea

In 2005, 342 cases of gonorrhoea were notified in Ireland. This figure is suspected to be well below the actual figure because 86 per cent of women and 55 per cent of men with gonorrhoea show no symptoms.

Symptoms
Many people with gonorrhoea don't experience any symptoms, but they can infect others. Symptoms in women include yellow or bloody discharge, bleeding during vaginal sex, bleeding between periods and a burning sensation during urination. Men may experience a white or yellow discharge from the penis, a burning sensation when urinating and sometimes sore and swollen testicles. If gonorrhoea has been transmitted during anal sex then there may be pain, bleeding and itching during bowel movements. If transmitted during oral sex a sore throat may result. If it is left untreated both men and women can experience fertility problems.

Gonorrhoea can be transmitted from an infected mother to her baby during vaginal childbirth. The baby may develop blindness, joint infection or a life-threatening blood infection.

Treatment
Antibiotics.

Chlamydia

Chlamydia is the most common bacterial sexually transmitted infection in Ireland with, for example, 3,353 new cases being notified in 2005. Like most sexually transmitted infections it is most common in the 20–29 age group (70 % of cases).

Symptoms
Similar to gonorrhoea. Babies born vaginally to mothers with chlamydia can be born with eye infections and pneumonia.

Treatment
Antibiotics.

STIs other than AIDS caused by viruses

Genital herpes simplex

In 2005 441 cases of genital herpes simplex were notified in Ireland.

Symptoms
Most people show no symptoms, yet are infectious to others. In those showing symptoms they

usually appear within ten days of being infected. Symptoms may include:

- Itching and/or burning sensation in the genital or anal area.
- Pain in the legs, buttocks or genital area.
- Vaginal discharge.
- Blisters where the infection entered the body: these later develop into sores.
- Flu-like symptoms.
- Burning sensation when urinating.

There is a risk of brain damage and even death to babies of infected women. Babies are normally delivered by Caesarean section so that they don't make contact with the vagina.

Treatment
There is no cure. Symptoms may be treated using anti-viral drugs such as acyclovir (brand name).

Ano-genital warts

Ano-genital warts are the most common STI of all, with a total of 3,456 cases being notified in Ireland during 2005.

Symptoms
Ano-genital warts first appear as small, painless bumps in or around the cervix, vagina, anus, penis or scrotum. They vary in size and shape and may not appear for several months after infection.

Treatment
The warts themselves often go away without treatment or may be removed using creams prescribed by a doctor. The virus that causes them, however, remains in the system for ever. This means that the warts can return.

Hepatitis B

There were 820 cases of hepatitis B notified in Ireland during 2006.

Symptoms
Hepatitis B is a serious infection that causes inflammation of the liver. It is a major cause of serious liver diseases such as cirrhosis and liver cancer and affects millions of people worldwide. The hepatitis B virus may be spread in a number of ways, including sexual contact with an infected person, sharing infected needles or from an infected mother to her baby during birth.

Treatment
While there is no cure for hepatitis B, anti-viral drugs may be given to help with symptoms. People considered to be 'at risk' from hepatitis can be vaccinated against it, e.g. health care and emergency professionals, family of hepatitis B sufferers, tattoo artists, etc.

STIs caused by fungi
The most common STI caused by a fungus is candidiasis or thrush. In men there are usually no symptoms, while in women there will be vaginal itching and a thick creamy white discharge. Thrush is treated with antibiotic creams or a vaginal pessary (capsule of cream) which is placed high up in the vagina using an applicator. These can be purchased over the counter in pharmacies.

Conditions caused by parasites
Parasites are tiny creatures that live off humans and animals. Pubic lice and scabies are common examples. Both will cause itching in the pubic area and scabies will also cause a rash. Medication will get rid of them.

ACTIVITY

1. How can you reduce the risk of contracting an STI?
   _____
   _____

2. Explain the statement, 'When you have sex with someone, you are having sex with everyone that person has had sex with.'
   _____
   _____

3. Which STIs should pregnant women have themselves tested for and why?
   _____
   _____
   _____

📄 EXAM TIME

Social Education (2005) – short questions

1. A person with Aids needs to be quarantined.

   True ⬜   False ⬜

2. Drinking heavily during pregnancy can cause a baby to suffer from:

   Foetal Alcohol Syndrome ⬜   Spina bifida ⬜   Asthma ⬜

Social Education (2006) – short questions

3. Aids is caused by the virus HIV which attacks the body's immune system and makes it vulnerable to various infections. What do the letters HIV stand for?

   Human Immuno-Deficiency Virus ⬜
   Highly Infectious Virus ⬜
   Hereditary Immune-System Virus ⬜

Social Education (2007) – short questions

4. Which of the following is an example of a natural type of family planning?

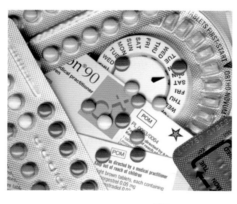

   Pill ⬜   Calendar ⬜   Diaphragm ⬜

5. There is an increased risk of heart attack and stroke for women who smoke and take the contraceptive pill.

   True ⬜   False ⬜

Social Education (2007) – long question (part)

6. Are the following statements true or false?

    A person does not die from Aids but from one of the diseases acquired because of the virus.　　　　　　　　　　　　True 　　　　False

    During pregnancy it is possible for a mother infected with HIV to pass the virus on to her unborn child.　　　　　　　　　　True 　　　　False

    Aids/HIV can be acquired by kissing an infected person.

    　　　　　　　　　　　　True 　　　　False

Social Education (2008) – short questions

7. The female reproductive cell is called the:

    Ovary 　　　Ovum 　　　Sperm

8. Which of the following lists contains three examples of sexually transmitted infections/diseases (STIs/STDs)?

List 1	List 2	List 3
Gonorrhoea	Cirrhosis	Emphysema
Syphilis	Chlamydia	Gonorrhoea
Chlamydia	Gout	Syphilis
☐	☐	☐

Module TWO

My Community

This module should be completed during session 1 (Year 1).

Below are seven key assignments for this module. You should choose FOUR of these. One of them must be a group activity and one must be an out-of-school activity. As you work through the module and complete the assignments you have chosen, come back to this page and tick off each of them.

1. I contributed several images/newspaper cuttings to a class collage about our local area.

   Date: ___ /___ /_____

2. I took part in a class discussion about our local area in the past. I made at least three contributions to this discussion.

   Date: ___ /___ /_____

3. I interviewed a senior citizen from my local community about life in the past.

   Date: ___ /___ /_____

4. I designed and presented a simple leaflet about five different organisations providing a service for young people in my area.

   Date: ___ /___ /_____

5. I plotted a long-distance journey by road on a map from my home to another point more than one hundred kilometres away. On this map I marked in the major towns, the distances to them and between them. I also showed an alternative route to this point using a different mode of transport.

   Date: ___ /___ /_____

6. I went to my local library and got the names of at least five useful resources/books on the history of my area.

   Date: ___ /___ /_____

7. I plotted on a map the litter bins provided by the local authority/authorities on my route to school.

   Date: ___ /___ /_____

UNIT 1 Research Skills

One of the features of the Leaving Certificate Applied programme is that it encourages you to find out things for yourself. To be able to do this you need to develop research skills. In this unit you will be looking at a number of different research methods. Throughout the two years you will be able to use these methods in all your subjects. The methods that will be looked at in this chapter are:

- Surveys
- Questionnaires
- Interviews.

Other sources of information are your school or local library and of course the Internet.

You will also be looking at how the information you gather can be presented by creating charts and tables.

Surveys

Surveys are used when you do not want very detailed information. Because surveys are generally conducted on the spot they cannot be very long or complicated. Surveys give the researcher a general picture and generally consist of only one or two questions.

Stages in conducting a survey

You must think about what it is you want to find out about or test. This is called your **hypothesis**. Examples of hypotheses are: 'most students in our school/centre get here by bus'; or 'most people in this school come from families of three children or fewer'.

The next thing you have to do is select your sample. Say you were investigating the hypothesis that 'the majority of drivers in Ireland wear seatbelts'. It would be impossible to survey all the drivers in Ireland, so you must therefore select a sample and restrict your hypothesis accordingly. You could say, for example, 'I wish to investigate the prevalence of seatbelt wearing among a sample of drivers in Mullingar town'. You must be sure that your sample is not too small – if you stood on the main street in Mullingar and surveyed just ten cars you would not get an accurate result. The bigger the sample the more likely your result is to be a valid and reliable one.

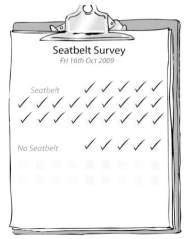

You need to have a quick way of recording results. A good idea is to use a clipboard like the one pictured. Once you have gathered your data you should count and present your findings. Pie charts are often used to present information gathered from surveys.

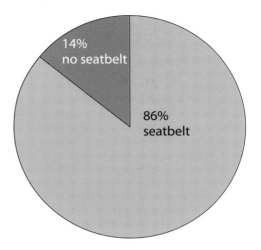

Percentage of drivers who wear seatbelts

Carry out a survey and present your results to the rest of the class. Perhaps your computer teacher could show you how to create pie charts like the one above to present your data.

Questionnaires

Questionnaires give us more detail than surveys and are a very common way of getting information about people's behaviour and beliefs. A questionnaire only works if the people who are filling it out understand what they are being asked and want to answer the questions being asked. This is why a questionnaire must be really well designed. If a questionnaire is badly designed people will either not fill it out at all or will be confused.

Designing a good questionnaire: points to remember

1. Only use one side of the paper.
2. Give the questionnaire a heading to show what it is about.
3. Give a paragraph of introduction at the beginning of the questionnaire.
4. Give clear instructions in bold capitals, e.g. TICK THE ANSWER WHICH MOST APPLIES TO YOU.
5. Keep the questionnaire as short as possible. Space out the questions well and leave room for answers.
6. Avoid too many open-ended questions, for example:

What do you like most about the Leaving Certificate Applied? _____

If you include a lot of open-ended questions like this one, which you could get a hundred different answers to, recording and presenting your findings will be very hard.

7. If the matter you are investigating is of a sensitive nature, put the most straightforward, non-threatening questions first. Leave the more sensitive ones to last. For example, if you were asking people to fill out a questionnaire on alcohol misuse you would not open with the question:

Do you think you drink too much?   Yes ☐   No ☐

8. Confidentiality is very important. People who fill out your questionnaire need to know that you will not be telling everyone what they have written. It is a good idea to put at the top of the questionnaire:

'Do not write your name on this questionnaire. I would like to assure you that your answers will be treated with the strictest confidence.'

9. It is usually advisable to carry out what is called a pilot study. A pilot study is when you give a draft copy of your questionnaire to a small number of people. When they fill it out, they give you feedback. They may be able to point out to you questions they found confusing or other things they felt could be improved upon. You can then design the final questionnaire taking into account the comments you received in the pilot study.

10. At the end of the questionnaire you should write:

'Thank you for your help.'

⚙ ACTIVITY

LEAVING CERTIFICATE APPLIED QUESTIONNAIRE

Dear Fellow Student,

I am carrying out an investigation into levels of satisfaction among LCA students with the LCA course. I would appreciate it if you would fill out the questions below as honestly as you can. Do not write your name on the questionnaire and I assure you your answers will be treated in strictest confidence.

Yours sincerely,

Mark Carroll

Mark Carroll

1. Overall how satisfied are you with the LCA?

   (RATE YOUR ANSWER BETWEEN 1 AND 10 – 10 IS EXTREMELY SATISFIED, WHILE 1 IS EXTREMELY DISSATISFIED) _____

2. What do you like about LCA?

(PUT 1 BESIDE THE BEST THING, 2 BESIDE THE NEXT BEST, ETC.)

You get marks as you go along – so not everything depends on exams ☐

I find the new subjects interesting ☐

I like the way subjects are relevant to our lives ☐

Things like work experience prepare us for life after school ☐

I get a sense of achievement from completing tasks and key assignments ☐

We don't get much homework ☐

We get to know our teachers well ☐

Other (please specify) _____

_____

3. Is there anything you don't like about LCA? (PLEASE TICK)

Tasks are too much work ☐

People don't know much about LCA and so don't think it is as good as

the established LC ☐

There is not much subject choice ☐

Other (please specify) _____

_____

4. What is your favourite LCA subject? _____

5. Why? _____

_____

_____

Thank you for taking the time to fill out this questionnaire.

Interviewing

Interviewing is another popular method of getting information from people. The main advantage of interviewing is that unlike surveys and questionnaires you can get very detailed information. The main disadvantage is that interviewing is very time-consuming and so you can only have a small sample. This could affect the accuracy of the results.

Preparing to interview someone

1. Think about what information you need and then set out the questions you wish to ask in a logical way.

2. You could do a practice or pilot interview with a member of your own group.

3. It is usually best to tape the interview so that you are not interrupting the conversation trying to take notes. You will have to ask the interviewee if this is OK.

4. Contact the person and, if they agree to be interviewed, set a time and a place to conduct the interview.

5. Start the interview by telling the person what your project is about and why you are interviewing them.

6. Begin the interview with easy, non-threatening questions; leave the sensitive ones, if there are any, until last.

7. At the end of the interview thank the person for their time.

8. Listen to your tape as soon as possible after the interview. Write out what was said. This is called transcription. Transcriptions are frequently put in the appendix of a piece of research.

 CD - Track 8

On Track 8 you will hear an interview. Lorna, the interviewer, is interested in music and would like to be a DJ when she leaves school. She is interviewing a DJ from a local radio station about his job. His name is Joseph Ryan. Listen to the interview three or four times and make a rough transcription of what is said on a sheet of paper. You will have to stop and start Track 8 to do this.

Presenting Research Results: Creating Charts

When you have completed your research and come up with a set of results you must now present it in a way that is attractive, interesting to look at and easy to understand. Below are some of the ways information can be presented:

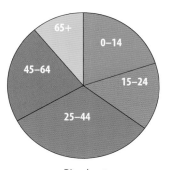

Population of Ireland by age, 2006
(Central Statistics Office)

Pie chart

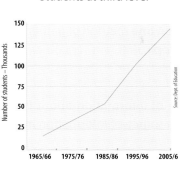

Students at third level

Line graph

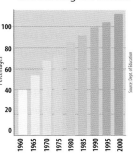

Percentage of students doing
the Leaving Certificate

Bar chart

Percentages of drivers who wear seatbelts

Year	Females %	Males %	Overall %
2006	92	82	86
2005	92	83	86
2003	90	82	85
2002	80	66	71
1999	68	48	55
1991	60	49	52

Table

⚙ ACTIVITY

Approximately what percentage of pupils entering secondary school in 1960 went on to do their Leaving Certificate? _____

What percentage of the Irish population is aged between 25 and 44? _____

What was the percentage increase in overall seatbelt wearing levels between 1991 and 2006? _____

Approximately how many people were in third-level education in 2005/6? _____

EXAM TIME

Social Education 2006 – long question (part)

1. (a) When researching information on the Internet many people use a 'search engine'. Name **one** 'search engine'. _____

(b) Name and explain **one** method of gathering information about people's opinions on a particular topic.

Method: _____

Explain: _____

(c) List **one** source of information about life in your community in the past and explain why this source of information might be used.

Source: _____

Explain: _____

Social Education 2007 – short questions

2. When doing a survey a hypothesis is:

(a) What you want to find out about or test

(b) The sample group being tested

(c) The results/findings of the survey

Social Education 2007 – long question (part)

3.

Year	Total	Males	Females
1951	2,960,593	1,506,597	1,453,996
1961	2,818,341	1,416,549	1,401,792
1971	2,978,248	1,495,760	1,482,488
1981	3,443,405	1,729,354	1,714,051
1991	3,525,719	1,753,418	1,772,301
1996	3,626,087	1,800,232	1,825,855
2002	3,917,203	1,946,164	1,971,039

(Source: CSO)

Population of Ireland 1951–2002

(a) Has the population of Ireland increased or decreased from 1971 to 2002?
_____

(b) In what year did the population of Ireland decrease? _____

(c) Outline **two** effects that an increase in population would have on your community.
_____
_____

4. Why is it important to use *'closed questions'* in a questionnaire?
_____
_____

5. Suggest **one** reason why a person would present the results of research on a graph.
_____

Social Education 2008 – short questions

6. What percentage of students go to school with a packed lunch?

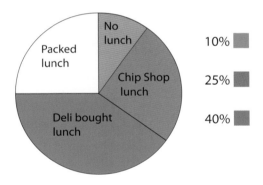

10% ▨

25% ▨

40% ▨

UNIT 2 My Own Place

It is well known that for humans to be content within themselves they need a sense of place. You only have to consider the number of people of Irish descent that come here searching for their roots every year to see that knowing where you come from is very important to people.

ACTIVITY

On the map of Ireland:

1. Circle the town you live in or the nearest town to you in red pen.

2. Draw a line showing your county boundary.

3. Name the counties touching the county in which you live.

    _____

    _____

4. Mark in blue and name the river nearest to where you live.

5. Name the mountain range that is nearest to where you live.

6. In blue pen, circle on the map three towns close to where you live.

7. Name a lake close to your school/centre.

    _____

8. Can your town or area be easily accessed by any of the following?

Sea	Yes	No
Air	Yes	No
Rail	Yes	No

The map for the activity above gives a general idea of where you live and what geographical features there are in your area. If you want to look more closely at an area you need a much more detailed map. These maps are called Ordnance Survey maps because they are produced by the Ordnance Survey Office in the Phoenix Park in Dublin. Ordnance Survey maps can be very detailed. The map you will be working on next has a scale of 1000:1. This means that every millimetre on the map represents one metre in reality.

⚙ ACTIVITY

On the map on the next page, find out the answers to the following questions.

1. Imagine you live at 2 Beechwood Drive. What type of house do you live in?

    _____

2. Name two other house types shown on the map.

    (1) _____ (2) _____

3. Imagine you live at 7 Marian Road. What house numbers are either side of you?

    _____

4. What is between 18 Marian Road and the children's playground? _____

5. What is opposite 16 Main Street? _____

6. Number 3 Chapel Street is a chip shop. If there is a fire in the chip shop where would the fire brigade hook up their equipment? _____

7. You live at 15 Beechwood Drive. Using the scale at the bottom of the map and a piece of paper, calculate how far you would have to travel to the bank.

8. Name three recreational facilities on the map.

_____

_____

_____

9. What type of area is represented on the map? (Tick one)

(1) A large town ☐   (3) A new urban development ☐

(2) A section of a city ☐   (4) A small rural town ☐

Give a reason for your choice.

_____

10. Think of one advantage of living in an area like this.

_____

Scale 1mm: 1 metre

Key or legend
Mh manhole
LS lamp standard
H fire hydrant
LB letterbox
TK telephone kiosk
P.O. post office
LC crossing

ACTIVITY

1. Using the website www.osismartmaps.ie/ find a map showing where you live or go to school. When you first log onto the site you will have to register with a user name and give your email address in order to be able to see the maps. Once you have registered click on 'browse maps' to find the map you are looking for.

2. Below is a section of an Irish road map. Imagine you are travelling by car from Cork city to Arklow town. List the villages and towns you would pass through.

_____
_____
_____

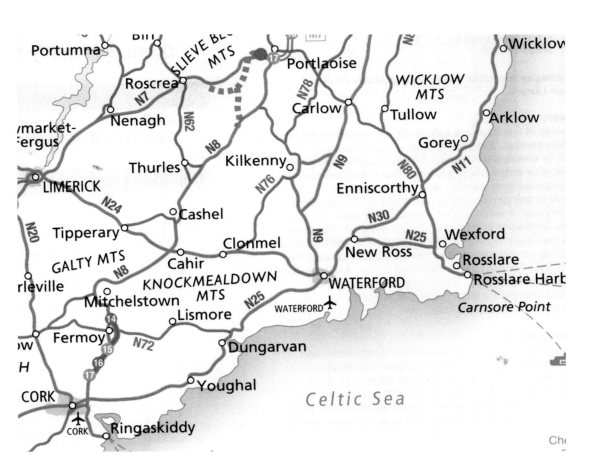

KEY ASSIGNMENT

For this key assignment you must plot on a map a long-distance journey by road from your home to another point more than one hundred kilometres away. (Some tourist offices supply free road maps.) On this map, mark in the major towns and the distances to and between them. You must also explain how you could make the journey using a different mode of transport. Use the route planner facility on the website at www.aaroadwatch.ie to plot this or another journey.

When you have completed this key assignment, go to the beginning of this module and tick it off on the checklist.

The Census

A census is conducted in this country normally every five years. On the night of the census every household must fill in the census form, giving details of everyone staying in that house that night. The purpose of a census is to get accurate information about the people of our country. This information is then used to plan government services and policies. All information written on the census form is treated in the strictest confidence. It is compulsory to participate in the census and failure to do so can result in a fine. The results of the census are usually made available to the public about one year after the census was conducted. They can be studied in the county library, but cannot be removed from there. Census results can also be downloaded from the Central Statistics Office website at www.cso.ie.

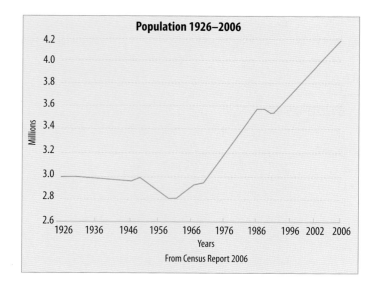

From Census Report 2006

The census tries to get an accurate picture of trends such as:

Overall population

The 2006 population figure of over 4.2 million is the highest since 1871.

Population of different areas

- Geographic distribution (what areas are heavily populated and what areas are not).
- Age and sex composition of population.
- Marital status.
- Living arrangements, e.g. numbers of lone parents, cohabiting couples, old people living alone, etc.

The census, as you can imagine, contains a huge amount of data, so is usually contained in several volumes or books.

 **ACTIVITY**

The census contains information on the population and area of each province, county, city, urban area, rural area and electoral division.

Here is the information collected for the 2002 and 2006 censuses for Inishowen rural area in County Donegal.

Population and area of each Province, County, City, urban area, rural area and Electoral Division, 2002 and 2006

District		2002	2006		Change in population 2002–2006		Area hectares
		Persons	Persons	Male	Female	Actual	percentage	
Donegal County (contd). Inishowen rural area (contd).								
073	Castlecary	542	666	331	335	124	22.9	2,054
074	Castlforward	913	909	465	444	-4	-0.4	2,277
075	Cludaff	841	899	467	432	58	6.9	2,599
076	Desertegny	682	662	335	327	-20	-2.9	3,072
077	Dunaff	653	663	339	324	10	1.5	2,729
078	Fahan	1,316	1,476	735	741	160	12.2	2,989
079	Glennagannon	606	671	342	329	65	10.7	2,056
080	Gleneely	693	746	388	358	53	7.6	4,090
081	Glentogher	980	1,133	533	600	153	15.6	4,193
082	Greencastle	747	807	402	405	60	8.0	3,387
083	Illies	738	796	398	398	58	7.9	4,881
084	Inch Island	438	438	219	219	–	–	1,386
085	Kilderry	1,367	1,744	901	843	377	27.6	3,088
086	Kilea	1,190	1,547	789	758	357	30.0	3,179
087	Malin	556	622	312	310	66	11.9	2,790
088	Mintiaghs	707	797	422	375	90	12.7	3,054
089	Moville	2,279	2,174	1,101	1,073	-105	-4.6	1,834
090	N'towncunnighham	769	1,178	598	580	409	53.2	2,004
091	Redcastle	638	791	422	369	153	24.0	2,952
092	Straid	1,254	1,344	698	646	90	7.2	3,565
093	Three Trees	551	646	318	328	95	17.2	2,841
094	Turmone	309	297	144	153	-12	-3.9	2,591
095	Whitecastle	699	883	442	441	184	26.3	2,902

1. Use the census figures above to find out which area has seen the biggest actual increase in population from 2002 to 2006. _____

2. How many females were present in Three Trees on the night of the census 2006? _____

3. Which area saw the biggest actual decrease in population between 2002 and 2006? _____

4. Which of the areas listed is the biggest in terms of area? _____

ACTIVITY

Go to your local library or look up the Central Statistics Office website at www.cso.ie and find out the following information about the population of your county and area.

Note: Volume 1 – Population Classified by Area will give this information.

1. What is the present (last census) population of your county? _____
2. What is the present (last census) population of your area (i.e. town, village)? _____

3. Has the population of your area increased or decreased between the last two census?
    Increased ▢   Decreased ▢   By how much? _____
4. Can you give a possible reason for the increase/decrease in population?
    _____
    _____

EXAM TIME

Social Education (2005) – short questions

1. In map reading a Legend is:
    A sketch of the area highlighting the main features   ▢
    A story of folklore about the region   ▢
    A list of keys describing features on the ground   ▢

Social Education (2006) – short question

2. In Ireland a census is generally carried out every:
    Three years ▢   Five years ▢   Seven years ▢

Social Education (2008) – short questions

3. Which of the following maps provides the greatest detail about housing and local amenities in an area?
    Road map ▢   Physical map ▢   Ordnance Survey map ▢

UNIT 3 My Family in the Local Area

Family History and Family Trees

The study of family histories and family trees is called **genealogy**. Some people find it very interesting to find out about their families in the past. During this unit you will have an opportunity to do some research about your own family. Find your family crest on the Internet. There are many websites that allow you to do this, and one is www.allfamilycrests.com/. Once you have found your crest why not print it, cut it out and stick it in the space below? If you cannot find your crest you could draw one that you think would suit your family.

Another interesting thing to do is to compile a family tree.

🔍 KEY ASSIGNMENT

For this key assignment you must interview a senior citizen from your community about life there in the past. You could interview one of your grandparents, for example. Be sure to have all your questions worked out before you actually carry out the interview. Here are some ideas for questions you might ask:

- How was your life at my age different from mine now?
- What was school like?

- What did you do in your spare time?
- How has the area changed?
- Would you rather be a teenager now or then? Why?
- Did many young people drink or smoke then?
- What age were you when you left school?
- What opportunities were available to you when you left school?
- My generation will all probably remember the attacks on the Twin Towers. What world events do you remember most?

When you have completed your interview and recorded your answers (keep these safe), go to page 79 and tick off Assignment 3 on the checklist.

UNIT 4 My Own Place in the Past

 KEY ASSIGNMENT

For this key assignment you need to go to your local library and get the names of at least five useful resources/books on the history of your area. Write the names of them below as evidence of having completed this key assignment.

When you have completed this key assignment, go to page 79 and tick off Assignment 6 on the checklist.

1. _____
2. _____
3. _____
4. _____
5. _____

KEY ASSIGNMENT

For this key assignment your class group need to make a collage about your local area. Each member of the group must contribute something to the collage. Photographs, postcards, press cuttings or drawings of your own can be used. Present your class collage on a large sheet of paper. Keep it safe as evidence of having completed this key assignment. Your collage could compare how your area looks now with how it looked in the past.

When you have completed this key assignment, go to page 79 and tick off Assignment 1 on the checklist.

ACTIVITY

Research some historic sites in your area. Write about your findings in the space provided. Stick a picture or a photograph of your chosen site(s) into the space below.

A historic site in my area:

_____

Newgrange is the most visited tourist attraction in Ireland

Stick a photograph or drawing here

_____
_____
_____
_____
_____
_____
_____
_____
_____

 KEY ASSIGNMENT

For this key assignment you need to take part in a discussion about your local area in the past. You must try to make at least three contributions to this discussion.

When you have completed this key assignment, go to page 79 and tick off Assignment 2 on the checklist.

ACTIVITY

Find out as much as you can about a famous person from your area. They could be a famous poet, politician, musician, sports person, writer, etc. They do not have to be from the past; they can be still living. Try to find a photograph to make your presentation more interesting.

 EXAM TIME

Social Education (2008) – long question (part)

1. (a) State **one** advantage of learning about the past.

    _____

    (b) List **two** sources that you could use to find out about your community in the past.

    1. _____

    2. _____

UNIT 5 Community Amenities/Resources

Areas with a strong community spirit usually have a host of clubs and organisations that are only too happy to have new members. In this unit you are required to find out about the various clubs and organisations that are in your area. Use the work card below to guide you.

 **ACTIVITY**

Think about the number of different clubs and organisations in your area. Look at the list and tick whether or not there are any of them in your area. Do not take too narrow a view of your area – this means within a few miles of where you live, not just on your doorstep.

Hobbies

Snooker	Yes		No	
Boxing	Yes		No	
Golf	Yes		No	
Pitch & putt	Yes		No	
Gaelic football	Yes		No	
Hurling	Yes		No	
Camogie	Yes		No	
Hockey	Yes		No	
Gym	Yes		No	
Basketball	Yes		No	
Tennis	Yes		No	
Fishing	Yes		No	
Badminton	Yes		No	
Swimming	Yes		No	
Children's playground	Yes		No	
Park or walkway	Yes		No	

Hobbies (non-sporting)

Gardening	Yes		No	
Bridge	Yes		No	
Chess	Yes		No	
Drama	Yes		No	
Music	Yes		No	

Charity work

St Vincent de Paul	Yes ☐	No ☐
Cerebral palsy	Yes ☐	No ☐
Barnardo's	Yes ☐	No ☐

Community welfare

ISPCC	Yes ☐	No ☐
Homework club	Yes ☐	No ☐
Parent and toddler group	Yes ☐	No ☐

Can you think of other clubs or organisations in your area not mentioned in the list?

_____

_____

_____

🔍 KEY ASSIGNMENT

Design and present a simple leaflet about five different organisations that provide a service for young people in your area. You could include the types of information listed below:

- Name of organisation
- Hours of opening
- How to become a member
- Address
- Facilities
- Fees
- Phone number
- Activities
- Equipment needed

You could ask your information technology teacher for help with the presentation of the leaflet.

When you have finished your leaflet go to page 79 and tick off Assignment 4 on the list.

Tourism in Your Local Area

Tourism is one of Ireland's biggest and fastest growing industries. Tourism currently employs over 245,000 people in this country and the number is rising every year (Fáilte Ireland). Certain areas of Ireland are well developed as tourist locations but others, while they have potential, are not so well developed.

 **ACTIVITY**

Think about your local area. Use the work card to report on what amenities and facilities for tourism your local area has to offer.

Natural resources

Rivers and lakes with facilities for visiting fishermen/women	Yes ☐	No ☐
Beaches with safe swimming areas	Yes ☐	No ☐
Mountains for hiking/hill walking	Yes ☐	No ☐
Forest walks and nature trails	Yes ☐	No ☐
Caves, waterfalls or any other natural attraction	Yes ☐	No ☐

Man-made attractions

Historic sites/buildings	Yes ☐	No ☐
Craft shops	Yes ☐	No ☐
Leisure complexes	Yes ☐	No ☐
Equestrian centres	Yes ☐	No ☐
Golf courses	Yes ☐	No ☐
Good restaurants	Yes ☐	No ☐
Good pubs	Yes ☐	No ☐
Good nightclubs	Yes ☐	No ☐
Museums	Yes ☐	No ☐
Art galleries	Yes ☐	No ☐
Tourist offices	Yes ☐	No ☐

Accommodation

Hotels	Yes ☐	No ☐
B&Bs	Yes ☐	No ☐
Campsites/caravan parks	Yes ☐	No ☐
Youth hostels	Yes ☐	No ☐

Transport

Good rail service	Yes ☐	No ☐
Good bus service	Yes ☐	No ☐
Is there much traffic congestion?	Yes ☐	No ☐

Other

Does your area hold any special events or festivals that would attract tourists? Yes ☐ No ☐
Is your area relatively litter-free? Yes ☐ No ☐
Is your area relatively crime-free? Yes ☐ No ☐
Would you consider your area to be attractive to tourists? Yes ☐ No ☐

Tourism symbols

General Facilities

km	Distance from town
C	Price reduction for children
	Open all year except Christmas
	Access for disabled persons
P	Car parking
	Central heating
	Elevator/lift
CI	Conference facilities
	Within 2 km of sandy beach
	Baby-sitting service
	Facilities for pets
	Facilities for guide dogs
	Credit card accepted
	Garden for visitors' use
	Family friendly hotel (facilities for children)
	Experience a working farm
Ir	Irish spoken

Bedroom Facilities

TNR	Total number of rooms
	Number of rooms with bath/shower and toilet
	Cot available
	No smoking bedrooms
	Light meals available

General Facilities (continued)

	Tea and coffee facilities
	Direct dial from bedrooms
TV	TV in bedrooms

Meals and Drinks Facilities

	Licensed to sell alcoholic drink
	Licensed to sell wine only
álc	Á la carte meals only
	Table d'hôte dinner

Sports Facilities

	Bicycles for hire
	Angling facilities
	Horse riding/pony trekking facilities
	Games room
	Gym only
	Leisure complex
	Outdoor swimming pool
	Indoor swimming pool
	Squash court
	Sauna only
	Tennis court
	Snooker (full size table)
	Golf

Using the tourism symbols and your own local knowledge, prepare and present a tourist brochure for your area. Include information on each of the following:

- Tourism attractions
- Accommodation
- Eating options
- Shopping
- Transport
- Cultural activities
- Entertainment
- Special interest activities, e.g. hiking, horse riding, golf, fishing, canoeing, sailing, cruising, etc.

To get this information you could visit or phone your nearest tourist office. The Internet is another valuable source of information – if you enter the name of your area/town and the word 'tourism' into any popular search engine, plenty of information and photographs should come up.

Your information technology teacher may advise you on how to improve the presentation of your brochure.

Industry in my Local Area

There are basically three different types of industry:

Primary industry	In years gone by this was a very common sort of industry. Primary industry basically means extracting the earth's natural resources and selling them, either direct to the public or to a secondary industry that will process them. Coal mining and growing crops are examples of primary industries.
Secondary industry	This type of industry processes the products of primary industry. For example, buying corn from a primary industry and making cornflakes out of it.
Service industry	This provides a service for the public rather than making goods. Tourism is largely a service industry.

ACTIVITY

List the main industries and sources of employment in your area. Place them under one of the three headings Primary, Secondary or Service.

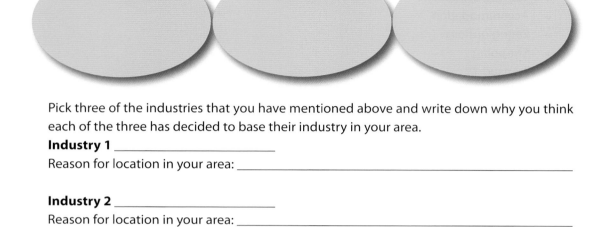

Primary

Service

Secondary

Pick three of the industries that you have mentioned above and write down why you think each of the three has decided to base their industry in your area.

Industry 1 _____
Reason for location in your area: _____

Industry 2 _____
Reason for location in your area: _____

Industry 3 _____
Reason for location in your area: _____

Find out what agencies promote industry in your area. Write down two of them:
1. _____
2. _____

Environmental Awareness

Today's society (both private and industrial) poses a grave threat to your local environment. Many people fail to see that environmental pollution and global warming, while they are global (worldwide) issues, are also local issues that will have a local impact. You as an individual should be doing your bit both now and in the future. Some things you could do include:

- Reduce carbon emissions – where possible, use public transport instead of private cars; do not burn coal.
- Save energy in the home – switch off appliances, e.g. TV and lights, when not in use; make sure hot water tanks are well insulated; use energy-saving light bulbs; take showers instead of baths.
- Reduce the amount of waste produced in your home – recycle.

📄 EXAM TIME

Social Education (2005) – short questions

1. Which of the following is a natural resource for tourism in an area?

Leisure centre ☐   Lake ☐   Golf course ☐

Social Education (2005) – long question (part)

2. In relation to **three** of the following environmental awareness cartoons, name and explain the method of protecting the environment that has been suggested by each.

1. Name: _____

    Explain: _____

    _____

2. Name: _____

    Explain: _____

    _____

3. Name: _____

    Explain: _____

    _____

3. (a) Mention **one** employment/economic activity situated in your local area.

    _____

(b) List **one** advantage of this activity for your area.

    _____

(c) Why did this economic activity/industry locate in your area?

    _____

Social Education (2006) – short question

4. Tourism is best described as a:

Primary Industry ☐   Secondary Industry ☐   Service Industry ☐

Social Education (2008) – short question

5. Fishing, farming and mining are all examples of which type of industry?

Primary Industry ▢   Secondary Industry ▢   Service Industry ▢

Social Education (2008) – long question (part)

6. Select either a social or an economic or a tourist amenity in your community. Briefly outline the advantage of this amenity to your community.

Social ▢   Economic ▢   Tourist ▢

(tick ✔ your choice)

Description/name of amenity: _____

Advantage: _____

UNIT 6 Planning in My Own Place

City or Town Planning

Planning began with the first towns and cities in about 3500 BC. Our ancestors set aside areas for housing, worship and other activities. They built walls around their towns for protection against enemies. Throughout history, people have done some planning for their communities. However, planning has rarely kept pace with the huge growth of urban areas. Many towns and cities have become polluted, overcrowded and have huge traffic problems. It is now the job of city and town planners not only to plan for the future but to repair the mistakes of the past.

Town and city planners try to predict the future. They attempt to forecast such developments as large changes in population and industrial activity. Town and city planners work for the government. They develop run-down areas and plan recreational areas, such as parks and green belts, and new industrial areas. They also try to improve road networks and parking facilities.

Most towns and cities in this country now have what is called a development plan. This plan is an overall vision for the community and is reviewed every five years. When it is being reviewed, members of the public can submit objections to it if they wish. Once completed, this plan can be examined in your local planning office during office hours. Closely related to this development plan is the concept of zoning.

Zoning

Zoning is a procedure that regulates the use of land. Town and city planners who work for the government divide up areas into different zones. Each zone has a different use, for example an area could be zoned as commercial, industrial, green belt or residential. Zoning means that towns and cities look more attractive, function better and are healthier places to live. Zoning also means that when you buy property, you have a good idea what building will be permitted beside you. For example, if you buy a house in an area zoned as residential, you can be pretty sure that a huge factory will not be built next door. Having said this, land can be re-zoned by your local authority. This could mean, for example, a residential area being re-zoned as commercial and a shopping centre being built on it.

 **ACTIVITY**

Visit your local planning office and ask to view the development plan for your area.

Objections to planning proposals

Sometimes local authorities make planning proposals that the local community feel would be detrimental to the area. Examples include large factories or roads, phone masts, landfill sites (dumps) and incinerators. Communities often come together and form pressure groups. Pressure groups can:

- lobby (put pressure on politicians for change)
- campaign (generate public interest by putting up notices, going on local radio, etc.)
- take action (organise marches and protests).

(See also Module 5 Unit 2 – Interest groups, page 209.)

ACTIVITY

How well-planned is your local town/area?	Yes	No
1. Are there good parking facilities in your town/area?	☐	☐
2. Is there bad traffic congestion in your town/area during rush hour?	☐	☐

	Yes	No
3. Is there a public park in your town/area?	☐	☐
4. Is there a children's playground in your town/area?	☐	☐
5. Is there a good shopping centre in your town/area?	☐	☐
6. Are schools situated near residential areas?	☐	☐
7. Do large housing estates have services such as shops, etc. nearby?	☐	☐
8. Are there facilities for Travellers in your area?	☐	☐
9. Have run-down parts of your town/area been redeveloped?	☐	☐
10. Are historical buildings in your town/area in a good state of repair?	☐	☐
11. Is there an industrial estate outside the town/area?	☐	☐
12. Is there a public library in your town/area?	☐	☐
13. Is there an arts centre or other cultural centre in your town/area?	☐	☐
14. Is there a public swimming pool in your town/area?	☐	☐
15. Is there a soccer or football pitch in your town/area?	☐	☐
16. Is there a leisure complex in your town/area?	☐	☐
17. Is your town/area bypassed?	☐	☐

KEY ASSIGNMENT

Draw a map of the route to your school or centre on a sheet of paper. On the map, mark in the litter bins provided by your local authority.

Put your work in your Social Education folder as evidence of completing the assignment, then go to page 79 and tick off Assignment 7 on the checklist.

Planning Permission for Houses

When is planning permission needed?

Planning permission is needed if you want to build something, e.g. a house, or change the use of an existing building, e.g. make your house into a playschool. Planning permission is not needed for small house extensions as long as they are: (a) to the back of the house; (b) under 23 metres square; and (c) not higher than the house. Planning permission is important because otherwise people could build what they want where they want and this would not be for the common good.

What types of permission are there?

- Full permission
- Outline permission
- Approval

To apply for planning permission you contact the planning authority for your area, i.e. county council, county borough, borough corporation or urban district council.

Full permission

This is the most common form of planning permission applied for. To be granted this, you need to know exactly what house or extension you want to build. You must submit the following:

- Application form
- Ordnance Survey map with site shown on it
- Detailed house plans
- Copy of the site notice (original must be posted prominently at the site)
- Site plan – showing where house is located on the site
- Advertisement from local paper, stating who you are and what you intend building
- Application fee.

Outline permission

People apply for this type of permission to see if the planning office will agree with their proposal in principle. Detailed plans are not submitted at this stage but at a later stage when full planning permission is being sought.

Some people go ahead and build first and then apply for retention afterwards. This is not to be recommended as you can by law be asked to remove the building.

Getting planning permission, if it is not objected to, usually takes three months from start to finish.

If you want to know more about planning, the Department of the Environment have published a series of 11 information leaflets on the subject. These can be obtained from your local planning authority.

📄 EXAM TIME

Social Education (2005) – long question (part)

1. Read the case study and answer the questions which follow:

> **Local Post Office to Close**
>
> It has been decided that Kilbally post office, which has been in operation for sixty years, is to close. Local residents will now be forced to travel six miles to the nearest post office. With limited public bus services this will make it increasingly difficult for the elderly who do not have their own mode of transport. An Post states that there is not enough business to retain the post office in the area. The local community plans to fight this closure.

    (a) Traditionally the main function of the post office was to deliver letters and parcels. List **two** other services that are now being offered by An Post.
      1. _____
      2. _____

    (b) Describe in detail **one** activity/campaign approach that the local community could undertake to prevent the closure of the local post office.
    _____
    _____

Social Education (2006) – long question (part)

2. Planning permission – fill in the blanks.

    • Applications for planning permission should be submitted to:
    _____

    • A number of items must be sent with the application form. One of these is:
    _____

    • Public notice of a planning application must be placed:
    _____

    • It usually takes about _____ months to get planning permission if no objections have been made.

3. The landfill site used to dispose of rubbish for your area has reached capacity. Your local authority has submitted plans to build a landfill dump in your area to replace the old dump.

Describe how your community could campaign to prevent the proposed dump being planned for your area.

_____

_____

_____

4. These symbols are often found on packaging. Explain what each one means.

a. _____ b. _____

Social Education (2007) – short question

5. Land zoned as residential by the planning authority will be used for:

   Factories   Houses   Leisure/Green Areas

Social Education (2008) – long question (part)

6. Planning permission is needed if a person wants to build a house. Why is this regulation important for a community?

   _____

   _____

Module THREE

Contemporary Issues 1

This module should be completed during session 2 (Year 1).

Below are six key assignments for this module. You should choose FOUR of these; one must be a group activity and one an out-of-school activity. As you work through the module and complete your chosen assignments, come back to this page and tick off each of them.

1. I took part in a roleplay (as a participant or observer) and recorded my observations about a situation where the denial of a human right was at issue.

   Date: ___ /___ /_____

2. I informed the class about a human rights issue/campaign I found in the newspaper or elsewhere.

   Date: ___ /___ /_____

3. I created an A1-sized promotional poster upholding one of the rights in the Universal Declaration of Human Rights.

   Date: ___ /___ /_____

4. I explained to my class three things I consider right and three things I consider wrong with regard to a particular contemporary issue.

   Date: ___ /___ /_____

5. I contacted an organisation/centre outside school that had information about a contemporary issue and gave a report to my class about what I had found out.

   Date: ___ /___ /_____

6. With other members of my class I organised a survey on attitudes in our local area to a particular contemporary issue.

   Date: ___ /___ /_____

UNIT 1 Social Context of Contemporary Issues

The third module in social education is called Contemporary Issues 1. During your study of this module you will be investigating and finding out about issues that are important to you. You will be asked to report back on your findings as part of the four key assignments. Before you begin this module, it makes sense to first of all investigate what the term 'contemporary issues' actually means.

Discuss with your class and with your teacher what you think the term 'contemporary issue' means. Write your definition below. Check the words 'contemporary' and 'issue' in the dictionary and see if your definition is a good one.

Our class think contemporary issue means:

_____

_____

As a class, brainstorm all the contemporary issues you can think of. Record what you come up with in the box below. A few have been written in to start you off.

Contemporary issues

Drugs	Gangland killings	Suicide

National and Global Issues

When you read an article about an issue in your local newspaper or listen to a discussion about an issue on local radio, you frequently see the issue only in terms of the problems that it causes locally.

Most issues, however, cause problems on a much wider scale. Issues grow to national and global importance.

Below is a list of local issues. Can you broaden them to national and global levels? The first one has been done as an example.

Issue	Local level	National level	Global level
Pollution	Opposition to new town dump	Pollution of Irish Sea by Sellafield	Hole in the ozone layer
Prejudice	Refugee is in hospital after racist attack		
Homelessness	Homeless man dies of exposure		
Drug abuse	Used needles found in kids' playground		
Conflict	Feuding families disturb peace with street brawl at two in the morning		

Note: For your contemporary issue task next year you will be required to look at the issue you choose to investigate from a local, national and global perspective.

UNIT 2 Forces/Interests

Local Issues Explored

Read the articles below, which are taken from provincial newspapers. When you have read the articles, answer the questions on them.

Athlone Boy Burned while Sniffing Petrol

A 13-year-old boy is in a critical condition in hospital after he received serious first-degree burns while sniffing petrol in the Ashwood Grove area of Athlone.

The boy was on waste ground with a number of other young people when the incident happened at around 9p.m. yesterday evening, Sunday.

It is understood they were sniffing petrol from plastic bottles and using cigarette lighters to heat the liquid to make it vaporise more quickly, when some of the petrol caught fire and exploded onto the boy's chest and stomach.

Neighbours and Gardaí who were called to the scene extinguished the boy's clothing using a fire extinguisher and he was taken to University College Hospital, Galway where his condition is described as critical.

Gardaí are conducting an investigation into the incident and have appealed for witnesses to contact them at Athlone Garda Station.

---

1. The boy in this article has severe first-degree burns as a result of solvent abuse. Find out another possible danger of misusing solvents.

   _____

   _____

2. Where do you think the boys in this article should have been at 9 p.m. instead of on the waste ground sniffing petrol?

   _____

3. What do you think parents can do to prevent their children participating in risky behaviours such as this?

   _____

   _____

   _____

   _____

4. What do you think the community can do to prevent children and teenagers participating in risky behaviours such as this?

   _____

   _____

5. In any town you will have two types of teenagers – those who are busy every evening with schoolwork, football, music, running, etc. and those who seem very unmotivated and who hang around doing nothing and complaining that 'there is nothing to do in this town'. Discuss this statement with your class and write down your thoughts below.

_____

_____

_____

_____

Mayor threatens to quit FF over Ridgepool asylum row

The Mayor of Ballina says he will quit Fianna Fáil if a local hotel is converted into an asylum seeker centre. Mayor Padraig Moore has spoken out against reports that the Ridgepool Hotel, which is about to be sold, will be operated as a centre for asylum seekers.

He told the *Western People* that as far as he was aware, the Ridgepool Hotel is to be sold to Bridgestock, a company believed to be the third largest accommodation provider for asylum seekers in Ireland. It would be contracted to provide the accommodation in Ballina by the Department of Justice. No planning permission would be required for the operation.

Mayor Moore said he was against the development of an asylum seeker centre on a number of grounds. Ballina already has a lot of social problems. The suspected location for such a development is beside the town's largest income generator – fishing on the River Moy.

The Mayor also hit out at the lack of consultation with the local authority over the sale of and future development of the 90-bedroom Ridgepool Hotel. It was contrary to Government policy.

Ballina Chamber of Commerce has voiced strong opposition to an asylum seeker centre as well. Chamber CEO, Sandra Cribben, said 'Ballina simply could not cope with the resulting influx of people. The business community would unite with the town council to reject the plan.'

Mayor Moore revealed that Mayo is presently the fourth largest accommodator of asylum seekers in the country, with approximately 400 here at present. He said the Ridgepool Hotel would have capacity to accommodate over 300. 'This proposal has the capacity to make Ballina the second largest provider for asylum seekers in the country apart from Mosney, which accommodates in the region of 800.'

And he warned that there was ample capacity to increase the intake of asylum seekers in Ballina. The adjoining apartments would be an ideal prospect for

> extending the Ridgepool facility. The Mayor pointed out that Ballina has the largest unemployment rate in the country. 'We are looking at bringing in another 400 people at least who cannot work and have minimum income.'
>
> From the *Western People*, 25 March 2008

(This article is only an introduction to the asylum issue. Not all the answers to the questions below, therefore, are contained in the article. Further research will also be required.)

1. What are the reasons given by Mayor Moore for not locating the asylum seeker centre in Ballina?
   _____
   _____
   _____

2. Do you agree with his views? Explain your answer.
   _____
   _____
   _____
   _____

3. What is the purpose of asylum seeker centres?
   _____
   _____
   _____
   _____

4. Find out some of the reasons why people are seeking asylum in this country.
   _____
   _____
   _____
   _____

 **ACTIVITY**

Get a current copy of your local newspaper. Look through it and cut out and read one article that raises a contemporary issue of local concern and of interest to you. Talk about your article with the class.

Forces and Interests that Affect an Issue

With every issue there are forces and interests at work that affect them for better or for worse. Take alcohol abuse, for example.

Some forces that make the issue of alcohol abuse worse are:

- personal problems that cause people to drink to forget them
- drinking is seen as part of Irish culture
- drunkenness is largely accepted in society
- some publicans serve more alcohol to obviously drunk customers.

Some forces that help the issue are:

- self-help groups such as AA, Al Anon and Al Teen
- addiction counselling services provided free by the health boards
- alcohol-awareness programmes written for schools.

Interest in the issue

Taking the issue of alcohol abuse, give your opinion on each of the following questions.

1. Who is affected by this issue?

   _____
   _____

2. Who is concerned about or interested in the issue?

   _____
   _____

3. What interest groups or organisations speak out about this issue?

   _____
   _____

4. Do those most affected by the issue speak out about it? Explain your answer.

   _____
   _____

5. Who has something to gain by the issue remaining unresolved?

   _____
   _____

6. Who has something to lose by the issue remaining unresolved?

   _____
   _____

🔑 KEY ASSIGNMENT

Contact an organisation/centre outside school that has information about a contemporary issue. Give a report to your class about what you find out. You may find the list of interest groups in Module 5 on page 211 useful here.

Issue _____

Organisation/Centre _____

When you have completed this key assignment, go to page 113 and tick off Assignment 5 on the checklist.

📄 EXAM TIME

Social Education (2007) – long question (part)

1. (a) Name **one** contemporary national/international issue that has emerged in the last two years.

   _____

   (b) Name **one** group affected by this issue.

   _____

   (c) Briefly explain how this group is affected by/affects this issue.

   _____

   _____

   _____

UNIT 3 Making Links

This unit is designed to allow you to make links between various contemporary issues and your everyday life. You will be asked to carry out reading, writing and listening exercises that will help you see how contemporary issues affect you as an individual.

Racism in the Blood

Racism is part of Irish society. If you think that's painful to hear, imagine how painful it is for me to watch and experience. There is no reason why this deeply hurtful oppression need continue in Ireland. Eliminating it, however, will require us to move beyond being morally against it to understanding the real ways it affects our lives and finding the skills to work through it before we tear each other apart.

I have been hit while attending my local bank, stared at, shouted at abusively on the street, told to 'go home', and been ignored queuing in a shop while I watched others behind me be called forward for assistance.

A significant issue here is trust. Racism teaches people in the dominant group they need to be afraid – that the targeted group (Travellers, Muslims, Jews, Africans and Asians) are uncontrollable, untrustworthy and will try to kill them. We act out of fear by blaming them for our problems and keeping them out of our state and our lives.

While many say racism in this state is new, Travellers have been targeted for hundreds of years as violent, drunk, robbing, untrustworthy, cute, abusing the system and dirty. I'm sure you can come up with more.

We are hopelessly focused on the 'others'. For as much as there is a myth that black people want to come to Ireland because it's a wonderful, easy place to live, there are floods of black people leaving this island because it is such a hard place to live when you're black.

Although it is commonly believed that our economic boom brought a dramatic increase in asylum applications in the 1990s, people from Britain, America, Canada and Australia have persistently immigrated to Ireland since the formation of the state. All this time, Ireland refused to provide safety for refugees at all. Only our recent membership of the EU has pressurised us to meet our international obligations to accept and process applications for asylum. Otherwise, we would still keep them out.

While almost everyone is against racism, it takes strength and intelligence to genuinely do something about it.

The Irish Times

ACTIVITY

1. Would you consider yourself to be racist?   Yes   No
2. Do others consider you to be racist?   Yes   No
3. Why, according to the article, are people racist?

    _____

    _____

    _____

4. Case Study: In the past Peter Sweeney has worked on and off as a painter and decorator but has been long-term unemployed for nine years. He lives in a corporation flat in Dublin's North inner city. Peter is extremely racist and frequently shouts abuse at refugees and asylum seekers he meets on the street. It drives him crazy to think that non-nationals are getting welfare benefits or corporation housing.

    A. Why do you think Peter is so racist?

    _____
    _____
    _____

    B. Do you think Peter has any right to be racist? Explain your answer.

    _____
    _____
    _____

5. In the past Ireland was a very poor country and many people left as economic refugees for countries such as England, America and Australia. What do you think the term 'economic refugee' means?

    _____
    _____
    _____

6. Have you any relations who emigrated as economic refugees because there was no work here?   Yes   No

7. Some people feel that we as a nation should be particularly understanding and sympathetic towards refugees and asylum seekers. Why do you think this should be the case?

    _____
    _____
    _____

8. Comment on the heading of the article above – do you agree with it?

    _____
    _____
    _____

CD - Track 9

Listen to the news item on Track 9 and answer the questions below.
(This article is designed to introduce the drug issue; therefore not all the answers to the questions below are contained in the track.)

1. What was the total estimated street value of the three drugs hauls mentioned in the track?

   _____

2. Do you think that this is a major find? Explain your answer.

   _____

   _____

   _____

3. How and why do you think people get involved in trafficking and selling drugs?

   _____

   _____

   _____

4. Is drug abuse a significant problem in your area?

   Yes ░░░   No ░░░

5. If 'yes', why do you think some people in your area have become involved with drugs? If 'no', why do you think people in your area have generally kept away from drugs?

   _____

   _____

   _____

6. On a scale of 1–10 how important is the drugs issue to your daily life? Circle your answer.

   1   2   3   4   5   6   7   8   9   10
   not important at all   extremely important

   Give a reason for your answer

   _____

   _____

   _____

Civil war – a contemporary issue
Civil war means 'a war between citizens of the same country' (Oxford English Dictionary).

Case study: Rwanda
In 1994 an estimated one million people were murdered in Rwanda over a period of 100 days. Why did this happen?

Rwanda is a small, poor African country with a total population of around 8.4 million. The average life expectancy is 41 years. Rwanda is made up of three ethnic groups, the Hutu (85%), the Tutsi (14%) and the Twa (1%). The Tutsi have historically been the wealthier group, owning land, and the Hutu and the Twa working for them. Belgium colonised Rwanda in 1919 and began educating the Tutsi and giving them positions of authority. This worsened tensions between the Hutu and the Tutsi because it seemed as if the Tutsi were getting everything and the Hutu and the Twa nothing.

In 1959 the Hutu rebelled and took power, driving many Tutsi out of the country into neighbouring Uganda. Between 1990 and 1993 Tutsi refugees from Uganda returned to Rwanda and began to attack the Hutu. They succeeded in taking over the northern part of Rwanda as their homeland.

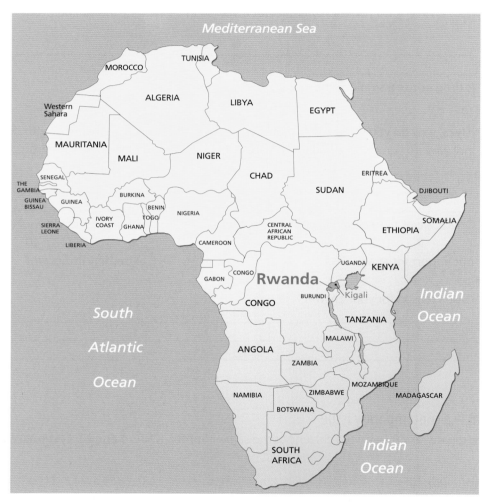

On 6 April 1994, however, the Hutu Rwandan president was assassinated. This sparked off a bloody massacre that was to last 100 days and claim over a million lives. Three-quarters of the Tutsi population was killed in a mass genocide. Many countries including France, America and Belgium suspected the genocide was being planned but did nothing. The United Nations, an organisation set up to prevent atrocities such as this, pulled out of Rwanda shortly before the massacre began.

ACTIVITY

1. Find out what the term 'genocide' means.

   _____

2. What do you think was the cause of the atrocity in Rwanda?

   _____

   _____

3. Why do you think the UN pulled out of Rwanda, knowing that a massacre was planned?

   _____

   _____

4. Why do you think countries like France, America and Belgium decided to do nothing about the impending massacre either?

   _____

   _____

UNIT 4   Contemporary Issues and Human Rights

The Universal Declaration of Human Rights

Background
On 30 January 1933 Adolf Hitler became leader of Germany. Once in power he and his party, called the National Socialists (Nazis), made sure that they took complete control. Hitler made it illegal for newspapers to print anything that went against him or showed him or his party in a bad light. It was illegal to hold meetings or say anything publicly that Hitler didn't approve of. Hitler banned any other political parties and so had total control. He then put together three police forces to keep this control. These forces were called the Gestapo, the SA and the SS.

Hitler and the Nazi party believed that Germans or the 'Aryan race' were superior to all other races and should take over the world. The Nazis saw Aryans as being typically blond, blue-eyed and tall.

The Holocaust Memorial, Miami, Florida

Jews were the first target of the Nazi hate campaign. Jews were not allowed go to cinemas, schools or even walk in certain parts of German cities.

Although the Jews were the main target of German Nazi hate, other groups such as Romas (gypsies), the handicapped and homosexuals were also targeted.

Between 1933 and 1935 Hitler introduced a number of forced sterilisation programmes, in which thousands of people the Nazis called 'inferiors' were treated so that they could not have children. Yet worse was to come.

In 1933 the first of Hitler's concentration camps was opened at Dachau, near Munich in Germany. Between 1933 and the end of his reign of terror in 1945 Hitler and his Nazi followers killed a total of 16 million people in these death camps. The biggest of the camps was Auschwitz in Poland, where many thousands were gassed, shot or simply allowed to die of starvation or disease. In some of the camps people were used as human guinea pigs for terrible medical experiments, which often resulted in the person's death. This reign of terror is known as the Holocaust.

When it was discovered what had gone on in Germany between 1933 and 1945, the Declaration of Human Rights was drawn up. It was written by a new organisation called the United Nations to guard against such atrocities ever happening again. The Declaration of Human Rights is really a list of rules that explain how we should treat others and how we should expect to be treated in this world. The declaration was passed on 10 December 1948. All members of the United Nations signed the declaration, with eight exceptions – six members of the Soviet bloc, Saudi Arabia and South Africa.

The introduction to the declaration states that:

> 'Principles of dignity and equality of all are the foundations of freedom, justice and peace in the world.'

Then 30 articles or statements are given. Below is a summary of them:

1. Everyone is born free and equal and should treat others as they would like to be treated.

2. Nobody should be treated badly because of differences in race, colour, sex, language, religion, etc.

3. Everyone has the right to life, freedom and safety.

4. Nobody should be made a slave.

5. Nobody should suffer cruelty or torture.

6. Everyone must be recognised by the law.

7. Everyone is equal before the law.

8. Everyone has the right to legal representation if their rights are violated.

9. Nobody can be unjustly imprisoned.

10. Everyone has the right to a fair trial.

11. Everyone has the right to be presumed innocent until proven guilty.

12. Everyone has the right to privacy.

13. Everyone has the right to travel within and outside their own country.

14. Everyone has the right to asylum.

15. Everyone has the right to a nationality and to change it.

16. Everyone has the right to marry if of full age.

17. Everyone has the right to own property and for it not to be taken from them.

18. Everyone has the right to freedom of thought, conscience and religion.

19. Everyone has the right to express their opinion without fear of punishment.

20. Everyone has the right to have meetings but not to be forced to join any particular group.

21. Everyone has the right to vote for whom they want by secret ballot.

22. Everyone has the right to social security.

23. Everyone has the right to work and to be paid equally for equal work. Everyone has the right to join a trade union.

24. Everyone has the right to leisure time and paid holidays.

25. Everyone has the right to an adequate standard of living with social welfare if you are unable to provide this for yourself.

26. Everyone has the right to a free elementary education.

27. Everyone has the right to enjoy the cultural life of their community.

28. Everyone has the right to social and international order so that these rights can be recognised.

29. The individual is entitled to their human rights as long as the rights of others are respected at the same time.

30. No country, group or person has the right to take away any of the human rights set out in this declaration.

 **ACTIVITY**

Read back over the account of the Holocaust and through the articles of the declaration. Can you think of eight rights that were violated by Hitler and his Nazi party during the Holocaust?

1. _____
2. _____
3. _____
4. _____
5. _____
6. _____
7. _____
8. _____

KEY ASSIGNMENT

Create an A1-sized promotional poster upholding one of the rights in the Universal Declaration of Human Rights.

When you have completed this key assignment, go to page 113 and tick off Assignment 3 on the checklist.

ACTIVITY

1. Describe briefly what happened in Germany between 1933 and 1945 that caused members of the United Nations to come together and draw up the Declaration of Human Rights.

   _____
   _____
   _____

2. In your own words, can you describe what the overall aims or principals of the declaration are?

   _____
   _____

3. When was the declaration signed? _____

4. In this country we take for granted some of the rights in the declaration. An example is the right to vote by secret ballot. This right is rarely if ever interfered with nowadays in Ireland. Other rights, however, are still being interfered with. In the space below, write down situations that occur in this country today where people's rights are not being respected. Beside the situation, note which article or articles deal with this right.

Example
Issue *Husband or wife beating*
What rights or articles are relevant to this issue? *Articles 1, 3 and 5*

Issue _____
What rights or articles are relevant to this issue? _____

Issue _____
What rights or articles are relevant to this issue? _____

Issue _____
What rights or articles are relevant to this issue? _____

Types of rights

Now that you are familiar with the articles of the Declaration of Human Rights, you will be able to see that there are different types of rights. These are:
- political rights
- social rights
- cultural rights
- economic rights.

 **ACTIVITY**

Show that you know the difference between the various rights by putting them into the correct box. Your teacher may need to help you. The first one has been done for you.

Political rights

Social rights

Article 1

Cultural rights

Economic rights

📄 EXAM TIME

Social Education (2005) – short question

1. The Universal Declaration of Human rights contains:

20 Articles   30 Articles   40 Articles

Social Education (2005) – long question (part)

2. 'The Universal Declaration of Human Rights (UDHR) contains the economic, policial, social and cultural rights of all people.'

UNIVERSAL DECLARATION OF HUMAN RIGHTS   Dignity and justice for all of us

A

B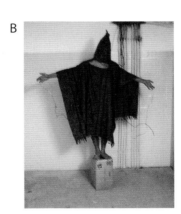

(a)   Select one of the photographs above (tick ✓ your choice).

A   B

In relation to the photograph selected state what human right is being denied.

_____

_____

Is this right

economic   political   social   cultural

(tick ✓ your choice)

Explain your answer.

_____

_____

_____

131

(b) Name a contemporary issue you have studied. Mention one interest group involved with this issue.

Issue: _____

Group: _____

Explain how this group affected the issue.

_____

_____

_____

Social Education (2006) – short question

3. A person who leaves their own country without hope of return and seeks refuge in another country is called:

A migrant worker ▢   An immigrant ▢   An asylum seeker ▢

Social Education (2006) – long question (part)

4. The following statements are examples of what types of prejudice?

No dogs or Irish allowed

Apprentice required – only male applicants may apply

Hey, granny! Where's your stick?

A. _____

B. _____

C. _____

Social Education (2007) – short question

5. The Universal Declaration of Human Rights was drawn up by the:

EU ▢   WHO ▢   UN ▢

Social Education (2007) – long question (part)

> *Bullying*
>
> Bullying can be defined as a pattern of behaviour whereby one person with a lot of anger and aggression uses their anger and aggression on another human being. This can take the form of teasing, criticism, verbal and physical violence. Young people in particular can be subjected to cruel and inhumane or degrading treatment in the form of bullying.
>
> Bullying at school is very common. Laura Grimes, a 14-year-old girl from Bristol, committed suicide after two years of ongoing bullying at school. She wrote a letter to her class saying:
>
> *'I suspect none of you are upset about my death, but I want to say I think I did this because of school and the bullies calling me fat and ugly did not help. I just wish it*

> *could have been different, but it's too late now. To all the bullies who made fun of my hair and weight and who I loved, you should never pick on anyone again 'cause this is what it does.'*

6. List and explain one human right that Laura Grimes was denied.

Human Right : _____

_____

7. Explain how Laura Grimes was denied this human right:

_____

_____

_____

8. List two positive things that could be done in your school to prevent bullying.

1. _____

2. _____

Social Education (2008) – short question

9. Which of the following is a basic human right?

A foreign holiday   Education   New clothes

Social Education (2008) – long question (part)

10. These Somali women and children have been displaced by fighting.

(a) Name **one** human right that these women and children are being denied.

_____

(b) Name a non-government organisation (NGO) that works with people in this type of situation.

_____

(c) Other than emergency aid, describe **one** way that non-governmental organisations (NGOs) help people in the developing world.

_____

_____

UNIT 5 Making Connections

CD - Track 10

Listen to the four news items on Track 10. For each of them, can you write down what human right or rights have been violated? Discuss your answers afterwards.

Item 1 What was the news item about? _____

What human right or rights were being violated or abused?

_____

_____

_____

Item 2 What was the news item about? _____

What human right or rights were being violated or abused?

_____

_____

_____

Item 3 What was the news item about? _____

What human right or rights were being violated or abused?

_____

_____

_____

Item 4 What was the news item about? _____

What human right or rights were being violated or abused?

_____

_____

_____

 **ACTIVITY**

This week, make a point of reading a local and a national newspaper and/or watching the news on TV. Pick three issues, one local, one national and one global. Think about each issue in terms of what human rights are under threat.

Local issue _____

Where did you see/read about this issue?

_____

What human rights, if any, are threatened by this issue?

_____

_____

National issue _____

Where did you see/read about this issue?

_____

What human rights, if any, are threatened by this issue?

_____

_____

Global issue _____

Where did you see/read about this issue?

_____

What human rights, if any, are threatened by this issue?

_____

_____

KEY ASSIGNMENT

Pick one of the issues that you came across while doing the last activity and that you found particularly interesting. Prepare a short talk to inform your class about it.

When you have completed this key assignment, go to page 113 and tick off Assignment 2 on the checklist.

 **KEY ASSIGNMENT**

Take the same issue, or choose another one, and write down three things that you consider right and three things you consider wrong with regard to this contemporary issue. Explain your ideas to your class. The example may help you.

When you have completed this key assignment, go to page 113 and tick off Assignment 4 on the checklist.

Chosen issue   Refugees coming into this country

Three things right:

1. It is right that everyone is equal regardless of the colour of their skin.
2. It is right that people should be allowed to get out of countries where their lives are in danger.
3. It is right that refugees should be adequately provided for so that they do not have to beg on the streets.

Three things wrong:

1. It is wrong to give abuse to refugees on the street as you do not know anything about them as individuals.
2. It is wrong that applications for asylum take so long to process, which means that the refugee must rely on social welfare.
3. It is wrong that refugees enter the country illegally.

Now your turn:

Chosen issue _____

Three things right:

1. _____
2. _____
3. _____

Three things wrong:

1. _____
2. _____
3. _____

UNIT 6 Understanding Concepts

Whenever the issue of human rights is discussed, certain key concepts or ideas usually come up. Below is a list of some of them.

ACTIVITY

Match each key concept with its definition. You may need a dictionary to help you.

1. A right	—	A. The unequal treatment of individuals based on age.
2. A responsibility	—	B. The unequal treatment of individuals based on their sex.
3. Democracy	—	C. Calm, quiet and free of disturbances such as war and riots.
4. Human dignity	—	D. The belief that human beings can be divided into races and that some races are inferior to others.
5. Interdependence	—	E. A country ruled by its people.
6. Law	—	F. Taking care of the world's natural resources, e.g. forests.
7. Ageism	—	G. Your duty to others.
8. Health	—	H. Something you are entitled to.
9. Justice	—	I. A group of people who differ in some way from the most common group in a society.
10. Sexism	—	J. The most powerful group in a society.
11. Racism	—	K. Having respect for others.
12. Prejudice	—	L. A state of physical, mental and social well-being.
13. Peace	—	M. Nations or people depending on each other.
14. Equality	—	N. The rules which try to control society.
15. Dominant group	—	O. Fairness
16. Safety	—	P. An opinion formed without full knowledge.
17. Minority group	—	Q. To be treated the same.
18. Poverty	—	R. Free from danger.
19. Environmental protection	—	S. In need, without enough.

Sometimes a contemporary issue arises where there is a conflict of rights. Look at the three situations below. Can you see that both sides have rights even though they conflict?

Situation 1
Rumours have been circulating around a small town that a certain man, let's call him Mr X, has raped a young girl in the local area. A group of people call on Mr X's home and beat him to within an inch of his life.

Explain how there is a conflict of rights: _____

_____

_____

Situation 2
A company owned by a man called Mr Y declares itself bankrupt and does not pay its debts to a number of people who have invested their life savings in it. Mr Y says that he cannot honour the debts. The people who are owed the money see that Mr Y lives in a big house and seems to be very well off. They want him to be forced to sell his house and pay them back their money.

Explain how there is a conflict of rights: _____

_____

_____

Situation 3
A second class teacher in a primary school refuses to have one particular boy in her class. The teacher claims that the boy is so disruptive that the other children in the class learn very little when he is there. Most days the boy is sent out of class and spends his time looking at the pictures in magazines. The boy cannot read.

Explain how there is a conflict of rights: _____

_____

_____

Watch one or more of the following films. Each of these films deals with examples of the violation of human rights.

Schindler's List	*Not Without my Daughter*
Saving Private Ryan	*The Thin Red Line*
The Color Purple	*To Kill a Mocking Bird*
Amistad	*In the Name of the Father*
Murder in the First	*Philadelphia*
Mississippi Burning	*Song for a Raggy Boy*

Note: Age restrictions may apply to some of these films.

Summarise what the film is about and what human rights you think were violated in the film.

_____

_____

_____

_____

_____

_____

_____

_____

_____

_____

_____

_____

_____

_____

_____

_____

_____

_____

_____

_____

_____

Human Rights Issues - Afghanistan

Brief history of Afghanistan

Because of Afghanistan's geographic location, landlocked with the former Soviet Union to the north, Pakistan and India to the east and Iran to the west, it has been constantly invaded and occupied throughout history. This has resulted in a country with many different warring factions or groups. The country has a long history of violence, with individual warlords trying to defeat each other in efforts to take control. In 1978 the former Soviet Union invaded Afghanistan (interestingly, the US government supported the mujahidin in Afghanistan against the Soviets at this time. The mujahidin later formed a large part of the Taliban). Many Afghans, especially downtrodden ethnic groups such as the Tajiks, Hazara, Aimaks, Uzbeks and Turkmen, rejoiced in the streets thinking that they would be treated better under Soviet rule. In 1989 the Soviet Union withdrew and there followed a return to civil war with the various factions in Afghanistan fighting in an effort to gain overall control.

In 1994 a number of warring factions, including the mujahidin (who, remember, had been supported in the past by the USA), came together to form the infamous Taliban, which took control of Afghanistan. The Taliban was composed mainly of the largest and strongest ethnic group in Afghanistan – the Pashtuns – and was led by 31-year-old Mullah Mohammed Omar. The Taliban considered themselves 'holy warriors' or 'freedom fighters' opposing the political and moral invasion of Afghanistan. Again, the Afghan people welcomed the change and cheered when the Taliban took over, hoping that the corrupt warlords would be put in their place and peace would be restored.

The Taliban passed a huge number of laws supposedly in the interests of Islam. These laws are the focus of this section, because they seriously impinge on human rights, particularly the rights of women. Examples of the laws passed and violently enforced by the Taliban include:

- Music, movies and television, computers, picnics, wedding parties, New Year celebrations, any kind of mixed-sex gathering were made illegal.
- Children's toys, including dolls, kites, card and board games, cameras, photographs, paintings of people and animals, pet parakeets were all banned.
- Cigarettes, alcohol, magazines and newspapers, and most books were banned. Afghans were not allowed to be with or talk to foreigners. Applause was forbidden.

Explaining why his regime banned virtually all forms of entertainment, Sher Abbas Stanakzai, who was the Taliban's 36-year-old deputy Minister of Foreign Affairs, said, 'Time should be spent serving the country and praying to God, nothing else. Everything else is a waste of time, and people are not allowed to waste their time.'

For women, the restrictions were even harsher:

- Female education was banned.
- Employment for women was banned.
- It was illegal to wear make-up, nail polish (for which the punishment was losing a finger) or jewellery, to pluck your eyebrows, cut your hair short, wear colourful or stylish clothes, sheer stockings, white socks and shoes, high-heeled shoes, walk loudly, talk loudly or laugh in public.

- Women could not step outside their house without a close male relative.
- If women did venture out, it had to be for an essential, government-sanctioned purpose, and they had to be covered from head to toe in a burqa.

The burqa is a garment that covers women from head to toe. The heavy gauze patch across the eyes makes it hard to see, and completely blocks peripheral vision. After enforced veiling, a growing number of women were hit by vehicles because the burqa leaves them unable to walk fast, or see where they are going. The burqa caused other problems. Veils were very expensive to buy. Many women could not afford to buy one themselves, and as a result whole neighbourhoods had to share one. It could take several days for a woman's turn to come round so even if she had money to shop for food, she couldn't go out until she had the veil. In most areas of Afghanistan outside the capital Kabul, women must still wear a burqa in public.

- The only public transport women were permitted to use were special buses, which were rarely available, and which had all windows, except the driver's, covered with thick blankets.
- It was illegal for women to talk to any men except close relations, which meant that they could not attend male doctors, and because of the employment ban there was a shortage of female doctors, so many sick women went untreated and many died.
- The evening curfew began at 7.30 p.m., after which no one except Taliban troops was allowed out, even for medical emergencies. Women in labour and needing hospital care had to remain at home until morning.

True Story

A young mother was shot repeatedly by the Taliban while rushing her seriously ill toddler to a doctor. Veiled, as the law required, she was spotted by a teenage Taliban guard, who tried to stop her because she shouldn't have left her home unaccompanied. Afraid her child might die if she were delayed, she kept going. The guard aimed his Kalashnikov machine gun and fired several rounds directly at her. She was hit, and died on the spot. The child lived. When her family later complained to the Taliban authorities, they were informed that the woman was at fault. She had no right being out unaccompanied in the first place.

On 11 September 2001 two planes crashed into the Twin Towers in New York and a total of 2,996 people were killed. The operation was believed to be the work of Osama bin Laden, an Islamic militant who believes that that Muslims should kill civilians and military personnel from the United States and allied countries until they withdraw military forces from Islamic countries such as Israel. After 9/11 it was thought that bin Laden fled to Afghanistan and that the Afghan government (the Taliban) were hiding him. It was not until this happened that the world began to focus on Afghanistan and its human rights violations.

US forces entered Afghanistan in October 2001 and within months had overthrown the Taliban. Elections were held and a new government was formed with Hamid Karzai as president.

Afghanistan today

In January 2002, George W. Bush said in his State of the Union address: 'The last time we met in this chamber, the mothers and daughters of Afghanistan were captives in their own homes, forbidden from working or going to school. Today women are free . . .' Most people now realise that this is far from the truth and that while the Taliban may have been overthrown, former Taliban members still live as ordinary citizens in Afghanistan and the country is still a profoundly male-dominated society where women are still very much second-class citizens.
Today in Afghanistan:

- Young girls (13 or 14 years old) are still forced by their families into arranged marriages – often to much older men, and often to settle debts or arguments.
- While in theory the ban on the education of girls and women has been lifted, in some rural parts of Afghanistan girls' participation rates in education are as low as two per cent, whereas participation rates by boys are consistently as high as 98 per cent.
- Women are still being arrested and jailed for 'moral crimes' or 'un-Islamic behaviour' such as talking to a male who is not related to them.
- Afghan women who campaign for change are frequently in grave danger and many have been killed.
- Instances of domestic violence are extremely high in Afghanistan and very few cases are being brought to justice. Suicide by self-immolation (usually by soaking themselves in petrol and setting themselves on fire) is very common among Afghan women and girls: many believe death is their only option. Some women commit petty crimes in order to be sent to prison, where they are at least free from abuse. In 2007, 165 women committed suicide by self-immolation (Afghan Independent Human Rights Commission).

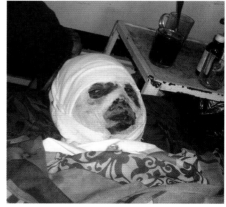

Unable to bear the physical, mental and sexual abuse she was subjected to daily, this young woman poured diesel over herself and set herself alight. She died within days of this picture being taken.

ACTIVITY

1. Why has there been a history of war and violence in Afghanistan?

_____

_____

_____

2. Why did the Taliban pass all their strict laws?

_____

_____

_____

3. Can you think of four human rights that are/were frequently denied women in Afghanistan?

    A. _____

    B. _____

    C. _____

    D. _____

4. Why did the USA invade Afghanistan in October 2001?

_____

_____

5. Why is it ironic that the USA ended up fighting the Taliban and defeating them?

_____

_____

6. Do you think George W. Bush actually believes that women in Afghanistan are now free? Why do you think he said this in his speech?

_____

_____

_____

7. Describe what you think it would be like being a woman in Afghanistan today.

_____

_____

_____

8. Name an organisation that concerns itself with human rights issues. _____

    • You could find out more about Afghanistan by doing some research yourself on the Internet. An investigation into the plight of women, not just in Afghanistan but in many other Muslim countries around the world, would make an excellent contemporary issues project next year.

    • The books *The Kite Runner* by Khaled Hosseini and *A Thousand Splendid Suns* are excellent books set in Afghanistan. The first is written through the eyes of a young boy and the second from the viewpoint of a young girl.

KEY ASSIGNMENT

For this key assignment you must take part in a roleplay (either as a participant or as an observer) where a denial of human rights is at issue. After the role play, write down what you observed and keep this in your Social Education folder as evidence of assignments completed.

When you have completed this key assignment, go to page 113 and tick off Assignment 1 on the checklist.

IDEAS FOR ROLEPLAYS

Immigrants
Roleplays might address how society at large sees immigrants; how you as an individual see immigrants; begging; solutions to the issues raised.

Unemployment
Roleplays could address why unemployment is a problem in Ireland; what groups most frequently face unemployment; the taxpayers' view of unemployment; people in employment claiming benefit and keeping it secret; solutions to the issues raised.

Sexual harassment
Roleplays could address what is meant by sexual harassment; sexual harassment in the workplace or around your peers; whether the harassers are aware of what they are doing; how sexual harassment is best dealt with.

Racism
Roleplays might address reasons for racism; who is racist; how do people show their racist tendencies; solutions to the issues raised.

Discrimination (class, sex, sexual orientation, religion)
Roleplays might address your own experiences of discrimination; who you as an individual discriminate against; who society as a whole discriminates against and why.

Disability
Roleplays could address problems with travel; work; how society sees disability; how you view disability; whether the benefits available are good enough; whether disabled people are treated as equals; solutions to the issues raised.

KEY ASSIGNMENT

Throughout this chapter you have looked at many different contemporary issues. With other members of your class organise a survey on attitudes in your local area to a particular issue.

When you have completed this key assignment, go to page 113 and tick off Assignment 6 on the checklist.

their say, without interrupting them. A lot of the time it is pointless trying to reason with them when they are in the middle of their angry outburst. You may even start to lose your temper yourself. This will end up with both of you going away feeling terrible.

Tips for dealing with your anger

- Get rid of the tension caused by your anger – run, go for a walk, do breathing exercises, write down why you are angry, punch a cushion.
- Tell the person calmly why you are angry with them.
- Listen to what they have to say.
- Work out together what you can both do about the situation.

KEY ASSIGNMENT

For this key assignment you are required to make a list/chart/collage/picture of different ways of dealing with anger so that the anger does little harm to you or others around you. When you have completed this key assignment, go to page 147 and tick off Assignment 1 on the checklist.

Receiving criticism

Criticism can be either constructive or destructive. Constructive criticism is not given to put us down or make us feel small but to help us learn and improve. Destructive criticism, on the other hand, is negative in nature and is not designed to help us. People who constantly put others down in this way are often unhappy with themselves and think that if they can put others down they will feel better about themselves. Of course they never do; if you put down others, it will only make you feel worse.

Destructive criticism

From time to time we all come across people who are very critical of others. They make hurtful remarks, which are not designed to help us in any way but designed to try to make us feel bad. If someone treats you like this, the best idea is to ignore what is being said and try to avoid getting angry.

Constructive criticism

Constructive criticism is always given to help the individual learn and progress. For criticism to be constructive it should always be (a) positive and (b) forward-looking, never negative and backward-looking.

Read the following examples.

A learner has made chicken curry and rice in cookery class. The curry tastes nice but the presentation is very sloppy.

Teacher A

The teacher tastes the curry and says 'Mmm, lovely. That curry really tastes great, not too hot – good job. Next time you could put the rice on the plate first and then spoon the curry neatly on top – that way it will look as good as it tastes. Well done.'

In this example the student is praised for what he/she has done well. The feedback is positive (what is good about the curry) and forward-looking (how they can make the curry even better next time).

Teacher B

The teacher does not taste the curry and says, 'The presentation needs to be much better: you should have put the rice on the plate first and then spooned the curry carefully on top. Food needs to look as well as taste good.'

In this example the teacher focuses only on what is wrong (negative) and is backward-looking (what the student should have done rather than what they could do next time).

 **ACTIVITY**

Write down what you would say to this student to offer them positive criticism.

A student writes a two-page essay for homework. The ideas in the essay are good, it has humour and he/she has clearly spent time on it. The essay, however, has no paragraphs, very little punctuation and is full of spelling mistakes.

_____

_____

_____

Dealing with criticism

- Think about whether the criticism is valid or invalid. Is it meant to be constructive?
- If it is invalid, it is best to stay calm and either ignore what has been said or tell the person that what they have said has hurt you.
- If the criticism is valid, think about how you can learn from it.

KEY ASSIGNMENT

Option A – Dealing with criticism

In groups of two (or three if you include an observer) choose one of the following roleplays, or create one of your own. You may like to deal badly with some of the criticisms, just to highlight the difference between dealing badly and dealing well with criticism.

When you have completed this key assignment, go to page 147 and tick off Assignment 2 on the checklist.

Roleplay 1	You tog out for leisure and recreation class and a member of your group starts criticising what you have on and how you look.
Roleplay 2	You have done a rough copy of your first task and your teacher is going through it with you. She is giving you constructive criticism.
Roleplay 3	You are going out on your first work experience to a solicitor's office and come into school beforehand dressed in a tracksuit. Your work experience teacher does not think you are dressed very appropriately and offers you some suggestions about what it would be better to wear.
Roleplay 4	You are going out on a Saturday night and are wearing a very revealing outfit. Your father takes one look at the outfit and starts criticising how you look.
Roleplay 5	You are playing a football/basketball match and things are not going too well. The coach gives you a lecture at half time about what you are doing wrong.

OR:

KEY ASSIGNMENT

Option B – Trying to resolve a conflict situation

For this key assignment you are required to describe a method of trying to solve conflicts.

Complete the activities below and then roleplay them.

When you have completed this key assignment, go to page 147 and tick off Assignment 2 on the checklist.

Place yourself in the following situations. Write down how each of the people in them could effectively control their anger, yet not passively accept the wrongs that have been done to them:

Sarah

Sarah, who is 17 years old, has been going out with Sean, who is 18, for the past four months. Today at school Mary, a fairly close friend, told Sarah that a girl in another class was seen with Sean at the weekend after the nightclub. Mary is fairly sure that the information is reliable and that Sean has therefore been cheating on Sarah. Sarah is furious. She cannot believe what she is hearing.

What do you think Sarah should do?_____

_____

What should Sarah not do? _____

_____

Patrick

During maths class Niall throws a rolled-up ball of paper at the teacher when his back is turned. The teacher opens out the ball of paper and sees that it is Patrick's work. The teacher automatically assumes that Patrick is responsible for throwing the ball of paper, and says that Patrick is to report to detention after school. Patrick is not very good at maths and frequently causes trouble in this class. However, this occasion is different as Patrick was for once trying to do his work when the missile was thrown.

What do you think Patrick should do? _____

_____

What should Patrick not do? _____

_____

Joan

Joan is 16 years old. Her parents are very strict compared to most of the parents of the other girls in her class. They have refused to let her go out on a Saturday night to an over-18s club in the town. Joan thinks that this is very unfair and that they are just trying to spoil the fun for her. Joan is going mad as it is nearly ten o'clock and everyone is meeting at 10.30.

What do you think Joan should do? _____

_____

What should Joan not do? _____

_____

Real-life situation

Can you think of a time when you were involved in a conflict situation with someone? Write an account of what happened and how you dealt with the anger you felt.

Decisions! Decisions!

Every day each one of us makes many decisions. Most of these decisions do not have long-term consequences and therefore we make them quickly without thinking too much. Examples of these decisions are what to wear or what to have for our breakfast. Other decisions, however, have long-term consequences and therefore require a good deal of thought before being made.

How decisions are made

Put it off
This is when you decide not to make a decision. The problem that needs to be solved never gets solved if you choose this option.

Follow others
This is when you allow peer pressure or other things like advertising to influence your decision. You make your decision based on what everyone else is doing.

Act on impulse/gut feeling
This is when you do not consciously think about the decision at all, but follow your instincts alone. For example, you grab a child before he or she runs out in front of an oncoming car.

Play it safe
This is when you choose the option that carries no risk. An example would be deciding not to apply to any colleges in case you do not like living away from home.

Think through
Generally this is the best method to choose when deciding important matters that have long-term effects. Using this method you weigh up the pros and cons and make your decision based on this.

 **ACTIVITY**

What decision-making methods do you think each person used in the following situations?

Case 1
Eddie and four of his friends hang around the back of the shopping centre on Saturday nights. Last Saturday Paul had some hash and made a few joints out of it. Eddie had never smoked hash before but decided to smoke some of it.

Case 2

Sean has been going out with Paula for five months now. Over the past few weeks he has gone off Paula a bit and doesn't really want to go out with her any more. He hasn't broken it off, though, as he knows she'll be upset and he hates that sort of hassle.

_____

Case 3

Jacinta has a young child called Brian, who is two years old. Brian pulls down a stack of CDs from a shelf in the sitting room.
Jacinta slaps Brian in the heat of the moment.

_____

Case 4

Debbie is 18 years old and is finishing her Leaving Certificate Applied next June. Debbie has approached the career guidance teacher for advice about careers. The careers teacher assessed her and told Debbie that her interests seem to lie in creative careers. Debbie decides to apply to do a hairdressing course at her local college.

_____

📄 EXAM TIME

Social Education (2008) – long question (part)

1. Describe **two** ways in which a young person might deal positively with criticism.

   (a) _____

   _____

   (b) _____

   _____

UNIT 2 Relationships

Types of Relationship

Throughout our lives we are constantly involving ourselves in relationships with other people. These relationships have different functions and we behave differently in each of them according to their function. We form close, loving relationships with family and friends and more formal, functional relationships with people like teachers, doctors and workmates. For any relationship to be successful there must be give and take. In this section we are going to focus on loving relationships and look at what we as people give to them and gain from them.

 **ACTIVITY**

Think of one loving or personal relationship in your life at the moment. Name that relationship below and then write down what you want from that relationship and what you can give to that relationship. You could focus on your relationship with a parent, sibling, boyfriend or girlfriend.

Relationship _____

Name three things you want from that relationship:
1. _____
2. _____
3. _____

Name three things you can give to that relationship:
1. _____
2. _____
3. _____

Not all relationships are as close as this; other relationships may be more superficial or not as deep. You have a relationship with a huge number of different people throughout your day. Examples include shopkeepers and school maintenance staff. Can you think of three such relationships?

1. _____
2. _____
3. _____

Skills for Healthy Relationships

 **ACTIVITY**

The following are 15 words relating to skills for healthy relationships. With your class discuss what you think each one means in terms of relationships.

- understanding
- compassion
- genuine
- honesty
- helpful

- co-operation
- kindness
- dependable
- admiration
- trust

- faithful
- humour
- confident
- respect
- empathy.

 **ACTIVITY**

All relationships, with the possible exception of your family, must be started. Every relationship, including your relationship with your family, must then be maintained, and sometimes relationships must be ended. Each of these stages are the subject of a letter on the problem page below. Give some sound advice to the letter writers.

dearTina

Dear Tina,

I have a Saturday job packing shelves in my local supermarket. I really fancy a guy who works there. He hasn't really spoken much to me yet, but has smiled at me a few times. I have a feeling he fancies me as well.

What should I do next?

Yours

Sarah

Dear Sarah,

_____

_____

_____

_____

_____

Dear Tina,

I have been going out with a lovely girl for the past three weeks. The problem is I am afraid she'll dump me. I have had other relationships but have never been able to maintain them for very long. The trouble is I tend to get too possessive and then the girl starts saying she feels trapped. I really want this relationship to work as I think I love this girl. Can you help?

Alan

Dear Alan,

_____

_____

_____

_____

_____

Dear Tina,

I have a 'friend'. Let's call her Anna. She is always running me down. She borrows everything belonging to me including my fellas! She tries to make me look stupid in front of others by making me the butt of her jokes. The trouble is I have known Anna since I was in national school and she does have some good points. Should I end this friendship and if so how?

Yours

Ellen

Dear Ellen,

_____

_____

_____

_____

_____

Family Structures

Over the last few decades the structure of Irish families has changed. Find out what is meant by each of the family structures listed below.

- Traditional nuclear family _____

- Extended family _____

- Lone-parent family _____

- Blended family _____

- Families headed by gay or lesbian couples _____

- Institutions (children's homes, convents, etc.) _____
  _____

- Foster families _____
  _____

CD - Track 11

Some young people, for whatever reason, do not live with their birth families. Every year children who are considered at risk are removed from their families and taken into care by the health boards. In the past, children's homes were very harsh places. Children were made to work long hours and discipline was very strict. Today, children's homes are much improved. This is not to say that life in care is always pleasant.

Listen to the case study on Track 11. What does the speaker find most difficult about being in care?

_____
_____

Becoming a Parent

Becoming a parent can be one of the most rewarding experiences in a person's life. Some psychologists believe that to reproduce is in fact essential to a person's feelings of having led a useful life, and that people who do not have children always feel that they have missed out on something. Having said this, every year children are removed by social services from their natural parent(s), because they are feared to be at risk from serious physical or psychological injury. Potential parents must be aware of the responsibilities that becoming a parent brings with it.

Babies bring both great joy and great responsibility

Responsibilities before and during pregnancy

It is the duty of every couple planning to have a baby to give him or her every chance of being born healthy and well. For the pregnant woman in particular this may involve certain changes in lifestyle and diet.

Diet during pregnancy

A woman's diet during pregnancy affects not only a woman's health but also the health of her baby. Poor diet during pregnancy has been linked with conditions such as spina bifida and other abnormalities. It is, therefore, the responsibility of every pregnant woman to ensure that she has a balanced diet during pregnancy.

Smoking

It is the responsibility of every woman and her partner, if they smoke, to stop smoking if they decide to have a baby. Sometimes the woman stops and the man doesn't, thinking that his smoking has no effect on the unborn baby. This is untrue; passive smoking harms the baby in much the same way. Besides, men should show encouragement and support for the woman by breaking their own smoking habits. Smoking during pregnancy causes the placenta to become less efficient, thus depriving the baby of oxygen. Babies of smokers are more likely to be miscarried or may suffer in the following ways:

- be smaller and weaker
- be premature
- be a victim of cot death in the first months of life
- have breathing difficulties, e.g. asthma.

Smokers' helpline: 1850 201203.

Alcohol

Studies on animals show that heavy drinking by either parent can affect the unborn baby. Male mice injected with alcohol before mating are more likely to father babies that die in the womb. It seems possible, therefore, that some human miscarriages may be related to the heavy drinking of the baby's father before conception.

Foetal alcohol syndrome (see page 65) is a condition that affects babies of women who drink while pregnant. Babies born with this condition suffer various degrees of physical and mental handicap. There are as yet no safe guidelines for alcohol consumption during pregnancy, so the usual advice is to stop drinking altogether.

Other drugs

Marijuana, cocaine, LSD, heroin and glue sniffing all affect foetal development, especially the development of the brain. Babies may suffer withdrawal symptoms at birth. It is the responsibility of drug misusers to seek help for their drug habits before conceiving a baby.

When the baby is born

When a baby is born it depends on its parent(s) for everything. Babies need someone to be there for them 24 hours a day. The parents' social life must therefore be seriously curtailed. Nights out become rare. Continuing in full-time education can be very difficult; childcare is very expensive and grandparents may be unable or unwilling to take on the responsibility of a small baby.

The cost of a baby

Babies are very costly. Many couples do not realise this until after the baby is born. For the average couple on an average income a baby means making many sacrifices. Spending on non-essential items such as entertainment, hobbies and non-essential clothing has to be vastly reduced. Some people may have no income other than that provided by the state. Providing adequately for a baby on welfare alone can be a very difficult task.

Responsibility for a child's emotional well-being

How a child develops emotionally and socially is hugely affected by what he or she experiences in the home. It is every parent's responsibility to provide a safe, stable and secure environment for a child to grow up in. Ideally, parents need to be confident that they can provide this environment for a child before having one. Routine is important in a young child's life in order to feel secure.

Helping your child reach his or her full potential

Babies and toddlers are very eager to learn about the world around them. It is the parents' responsibility to provide a stimulating environment for them. Parents should try to read with their child, play games, listen to him or her, go for walks, etc. When a child begins school, it is the parents' responsibility to support their child's learning at home. Parents who have problems themselves with reading and writing may find helping their child with schoolwork a daunting task. To redress this, many early school leavers return to education when they have young children of their own. For information on adult literacy services call 1800 202065.

ACTIVITY

Invite a young parent to visit your group to speak about their experiences. You will have to prepare for the visit very well.

Make a list of all the questions you would like to ask beforehand.

ACTIVITY

The cost of a baby
Price the following essential items in shops in your area.

1 medium-priced cot	_____
1 medium-priced pram	_____
1 medium-priced car seat/carry cot	_____
1 bottle steriliser (even if breast feeding)	_____
2 medium-priced toys	_____
3 cot blankets	_____
2 sets cot sheets	_____
10 baby vests	_____
10 babygrows	_____
2 snowsuits (or outfits suitable for outside)	_____
3 baby cardigans	_____
6 bottles	_____
4 packets newborn nappies	_____
Total cost:	_____

Note: This is a shopping list for a baby in the first weeks of life; more expense will follow as the baby gets older. If you already have a baby, maybe you could write about your experience instead of completing the next exercise.

Would you be prepared to...?

	Yes	No	Don't know
1. Give up smoking? (non-smokers skip question 1)	☐	☐	☐

	Yes	No	Don't know
2. Give up alcohol before and during pregnancy? (If you are male, reduce your intake in support of your partner?)			
3. Reduce nights out to 1-2 per month?			
4. Put your education on hold?			
5. Get up 3-4 times per night to feed the baby?			
6. Never lose your temper even if you are tired or irritated?			
7. Reduce your spending to essentials?			
8. Take responsibility for someone else for the next 18 years?			
9. Do you have the financial means to provide for a baby?			
10. Would you be able to offer a baby a stable environment?			
11. Would you feel confident enough to support your child's education?			
12. Would you have the support of family and friends if you or your girlfriend were to have a baby?			

 KEY ASSIGNMENT

For this key assignment you must list the main tasks involved in taking care of:
- a three-month-old baby
- a three-year-old child
- a ten-year-old child.

Many of the main tasks are listed in the box below. Pick out the tasks relevant to each of the different-aged children and write them in the space provided under each. Some tasks may be relevant to more than one age group.

When you have completed this key assignment, go to page 147 and tick off Assignment 3 on the checklist.

Sterilising bottles	Drying clothes	Tidying up toys	Preparing finger foods

Winding   Supervising bath time

Changing nappies   Making packed lunches   Helping with homework

Washing clothes   Making up bottles   Supervising toy clean-up

Reminding to wash teeth   Collecting from school

Bringing to school   Breast feeding   Top and toe bath

Reading picture books   Four-hourly feeds   Making breakfast

Involving child in housework   Helping child with toileting

Helping to wash teeth

Three-month-old baby

_____
_____
_____
_____
_____
_____

Three-year-old child

_____
_____
_____
_____
_____
_____

Ten-year-old child

_____
_____
_____
_____
_____
_____

Rights and Responsibilities in the Home

Often fights or arguments in the home arise out of a conflict of rights between parents and their children. As a young person you are probably more aware of your own rights than those of your parents.

ACTIVITY

Here are some examples of conflicts. What rights do parents have in these situations?

1. You feel you have the right to have your friends over any time.
    Your parent(s) feel: _____
    _____
    _____

2. You feel you shouldn't have to do much work around the house. After all, you don't get paid for it.
    Your parent(s) feel: _____
    _____
    _____

3. You feel you have the right to stay home from school.
    Your parent(s) feel: _____
    _____
    _____

4. You feel you have the right to stay over at your boyfriend's or girlfriend's house.
    Your parent(s) feel: _____
    _____
    _____

Problems in Families

From time to time problems arise in every family. When a problem occurs in a family, it is usual that everyone is affected by it even though it may seem to involve only one or two members. As a class, try to think of as many family problems as possible. Write down five of the ones you came up with below.

1. _____
2. _____
3. _____
4. _____
5. _____

For each of the problems that you have listed find out the name of either a statutory (government-run) or voluntary organisation that can help with the problem.

In the past, in Ireland, it was illegal to be involved in a homosexual relationship. Now it is illegal to discriminate against people because of their sexual orientation. However, it must be remembered that, just because the legal ban on homosexuality has been lifted, prejudice against the gay and lesbian community has not ended.

Homosexual acts are punishable by death in Sudan, Afghanistan, Pakistan, the Chechen Republic, Iran, Saudi Arabia, Mauritania, the United Arab Emirates and Yemen. Of these, three – Afghanistan, Iran and Saudi Arabia – are known to have executed homosexuals in the past 10 years.

ACTIVITY

The letter below has been submitted to a teenage magazine called *Attitude* by a young gay man. Read the letter, discuss it with your group and then, as a group or as individuals, write a suitable reply.

Dear Attitude

I am sixteen and gay and I go to an all-boys secondary school. It's not as though being gay is something I chose, and it isn't something I can change. The thing is I know my family will never accept me for who I am because they are so old-fashioned and they will think that it is disgusting and perverted. I feel really alone and unable to tell those nearest to me the truth. I did tell my best friend Paul the truth at the start of the year, but this has caused the death of our friendship. He became distant and we stopped hanging round together. He then proceeded to poison most of my friends against me and told all the other lads in school that I was gay and they bullied me to the point where I had to drop out of school. Six months ago I made a vain attempt at suicide trying to swallow as many pills as I could, but my stomach rejected them almost immediately. I made two more attempts and am growing used to damaging myself. The last time I tried my mother caught me. She doesn't understand what is going on and wants me to open up to her, but I am afraid that she will hate me. I know my father will throw me out of the house. I don't want to disappoint them and feel that I would be better off dead. Please help me.

Anonymous

Your reply:

_____

_____

_____

_____

_____

_____
_____
_____
_____
_____
_____
_____
_____
_____
_____
_____

Below is a piece written by a lesbian woman in her twenties. Read the piece and then as a group look at and work through the discussion points that follow.

The hardest part about being a lesbian for me wasn't admitting it to myself, but building up the confidence to do something about it. Being young, alone and a lesbian can be both confusing and scary. When I told my friends they were taken aback at first but they then guided me and pushed me in the right direction. The first time a friend took me to a gay club, I was overwhelmed by the amount of people my own age who had come out. I felt that I had finally found people who understood how I was feeling and wanted to help me fit in. Some time after this I came out myself. When I came out to my parents, they were devastated. My mother couldn't stop crying and my father wouldn't speak to me. The thing was they did not understand what it was to be gay and assumed the worst. With time, they began to see how my friends and my work colleagues totally accepted my sexuality and I think that helped them a lot. It was a while before they told my extended family, meaning my aunts and uncles. When they finally did, they were surprised by the slight reaction they got. Now three years on I have a girlfriend who they accept and like. I think for them, like me, the worst part was pretending it wasn't there, and not talking about it. But with time and patience, they grew to see it as a natural and positive part of my life.

Discussion points

- Society's attitudes to homosexuality.
- How are these attitudes shown by society (e.g. language used to describe homosexuals)?
- Your own attitudes to homosexuality.
- The difficulties that someone might experience in trying to keep their sexuality a secret.
- The difficulties someone might experience on 'coming out'.
- Homosexuality as a positive thing, e.g. the high levels of creativity among homosexuals.
- Homosexuals as parents.

EXAM TIME

Social Education (2006) – long question (part)

1. FEEDING   SLEEP   BATHING   NAPPY CHANGES

   Above are the main events involved in the daily care of Jack, a three-month-old baby. List **two** other things that his guardians should do to ensure that Jack is well cared for.

   (a) _____

   (b) _____

Social Education (2008) – short question

2. Persons who are only sexually attracted to people of the opposite sex are:

   Homosexual   Bisexual   Heterosexual

UNIT 3   Coping with Problems

During this unit you will be looking at some of the more common problems or difficulties that people may meet in life. You will be finding out what agencies exist to help people to cope with these life crises. You will be required to use this information to complete the fourth and final key assignment of this module. The following are the problems that this unit will address, although you may like to investigate others that are more important to you.

- Loss/bereavement
- Sexual harassment
- Addictions
- Mental illness
- Rape
- Eating disorders
- Sexual abuse
- Unexpected pregnancy

Loss/Bereavement

When someone close to you dies, this can seem like the biggest life crisis that someone can have to endure. This is because of the finality of death. Unlike other life crises, death cannot be fixed or put right; we can only cope and learn to live with our loss and grief.

Whether the death was sudden or expected, it is normal to experience a huge number of emotions and feelings such as disbelief, shock, anger, guilt, and sadness.

Disbelief

This is often the first reaction when someone close to you dies. The death seems like a nightmare, not real. This sense of disbelief can stay for a long time.

Shock

Shock is another common reaction. You may feel numb and stunned, and you may not be able to think clearly; everything is happening in a haze.

Longing and searching

Most people experience a sense of longing: to be able to speak or hear or hold the person one last time.

Anger

This is a normal response to death. People need to be able to be angry with someone for their loved one's death. They may be angry with God for letting them die, or with doctors or medical staff for not doing enough to save them. They may be angry with themselves or someone else for something they have done or not done. For example, if a child runs out in front of a car, the bereaved parents are likely to feel anger at the driver of the car.

Guilt

This is a very common reaction. People tend to go over events surrounding the death and blame themselves for not doing more to prevent it. They may feel guilty about not having spent enough time with the person, or because they had arguments with them.

Despair, depression, loneliness and sadness

Very strong feelings of sadness and hopelessness frequently follow a death. You may lose interest in everything and even the smallest of tasks takes a lot of effort, for example you may sit round the house all day without even changing out of your night clothes. Other symptoms of despair and depression are sleeplessness, loss of appetite, poor concentration and constant crying.

Physical reactions

When someone close to you dies, you may experience physical as well as emotional effects. Some common physical reactions are tiredness, headaches, sleeplessness, loss of appetite, pains in your muscles, pains or a tightness in your chest, nausea and diarrhoea.

Helping yourself through your grief

- Talk to others about how you are feeling.
- Don't cut yourself off from others.
- Give yourself time.

- Don't take comfort in drugs or alcohol; this is only masking the feelings, not dealing with them.
- Get rest and exercise; try to eat well.
- Write about how you feel.

Helping others through their grief

- Do not avoid the subject of the person's death.
- Allow the bereaved person to talk about how they feel. Don't keep giving advice – usually the person just wants you to listen, not to find a solution to their problems.
- Help by doing practical tasks, e.g. tidying the house.
- Allow the bereaved person to cry, and don't be afraid to cry yourself.

Where to go for help

The HSE offers a bereavement counselling service. This service is best accessed through a GP.

Sexual Harassment

Sexual harassment, in law, consists of deliberate and unwelcome sexual advances, unwanted requests for sexual favours, and certain other offensive conduct of a sexual nature. Sexual harassment may be committed by men or women in many different roles, such as that of boss, client, co-worker, fellow student, or teacher. However, a large majority of cases involve the harassment of women by their male bosses or fellow employees. Most countries have laws against sexual harassment.

The law recognises two types of employment-related sexual harassment: (a) quid pro quo and (b) hostile environment. Quid pro quo harassment occurs when a person in authority requires sexual favours from an employee in exchange for things, such as getting hired or promoted or not getting fired. Quid pro quo is a Latin phrase meaning one thing in return for another.

In hostile environment harassment, the offender does not demand an exchange. Instead, a pattern of behaviour makes the victim's job so unpleasant that their work is affected. The harassment may consist of asking for sexual favours, making sexual comments, telling sexual jokes, or displaying pornographic pictures.

Sexual harassment is not confined to the workplace. People can be sexually harassed anywhere from pubs and clubs to walking down the street. The reason why a lot of laws focus on sexual harassment in the workplace is that people's livelihoods or education can often be put at risk because of it. Many workplaces have a policy on sexual harassment. Policies generally define what sexual harassment is and outline how the company deals with complaints.

ACTIVITY

1. What kind of behaviours do you think constitute sexual harassment?

_____
_____
_____

2. What would you do if you were being sexually harassed in the workplace?

_____
_____
_____

Drug Addiction

In Module 1 we looked closely at some of the common drugs that are available in society today. We looked at the effects of taking these drugs. You should revise this section now. Addiction is one of the biggest and best-recognised effects of drug taking and it is this aspect of drug taking that we will discuss now. Frequently drug addiction or, more correctly, 'drug dependence' occurs together with or after some life crisis. It then becomes a life crisis in itself. This is why we are looking at the problem now in this section of your course.

The World Health Organisation in 1964 described drug dependence as:

> A state, psychic and sometimes also physical, resulting from the interaction between a living organism and a drug, characterised by behavioural and other responses that always include a compulsion to take the drug on a continuous or periodic basis in order to experience its psychic effects, and sometimes to avoid the discomfort of its absence. Tolerance may or may not be present.

ACTIVITY

Read the definition above a few times, then put it into your own words.

_____
_____
_____
_____

Physical dependence

Physical dependence occurs when the body adapts to repeated use of the drug. It is thought that some drugs actually replace our natural stress-defence mechanisms and therefore when the drug is taken away we have fewer stress-defence mechanisms than someone who never touched the drug, and can therefore suffer acute withdrawal symptoms.

Psychological dependence

Strong psychological or mental dependence is a characteristic of some drugs. This occurs because the user begins to associate the drug with mental well-being, with feeling calm and happy. The user then begins to think that they cannot have these feelings without the drug and so craves the drug and the feelings that it brings with it. This is psychological dependence.

Some drugs cause both physical and psychological dependence. These include:

- heroin
- alcohol
- barbiturates, e.g. sleeping tablets
- minor tranquillisers
- nicotine.

Others are thought to cause no physical dependence, although withdrawal symptoms can still be very strong. These drugs include:

- cocaine
- amphetamines, e.g. speed
- cannabis.

Tolerance

With repeated drug use the individual needs more of the drug to achieve the same effects. A tolerance is built up and may be caused by two factors: the body becomes able to get rid of the drug more quickly; and the brain adapts to the drug, so that more of the drug is needed to get the same effect. A heroin addict can take 100mg or more of heroin in one injection. This dose would probably kill a non-addict.

Withdrawal symptoms

Withdrawal symptoms are experienced when a user stops taking some addictive drugs. The type of symptoms experienced depends on the drug. Sometimes withdrawal symptoms can be very severe, as with heroin addiction, where chills, pains and flu-like symptoms are often experienced.

Sometimes a drug substitute is given to make the withdrawal symptoms less severe. In the case of heroin, the most common drug substitute is methadone. Many people involved with addiction services in Ireland, however, are not entirely happy with how drug addiction is being dealt with in this country. Currently there are approximately 9,200 people on methadone maintenance programmes in Dublin city alone. Yet only 23 residential detoxification beds are available in the entire country for those wanting to get off drugs completely. Amazingly, while €100 million is being poured into the state-sponsored methadone programme, only a fraction of state funds are being spent on actually getting people off drugs altogether. Many people remain on methadone for long periods of time – nine or ten years – a state-sponsored drugs habit?

Where to get help

Usually when someone feels they have a drug or alcohol problem, they contact their GP or family doctor who will be able to refer them on to a suitable service in their area. In addition, there are a number of self-help organisations:

Alcoholics Anonymous
Unit 2, Block C
Santry Business Park
Swords Road
Dublin 9
www.alcoholicsanonymous.ie/
Tel: (01) 842 0700

Al-Anon (for families and friends of problem drinkers)
and
Alateen (for young people, aged 12 to 17, who are affected by a problem drinker)
5 Capel Street
Dublin 1
www.al-anon-ireland.org/alanon.htm
Tel: (01) 873 2699

Narcotics Anonymous
4/5 Eustace Street
Dublin 2
www.esatclear.ie/~jackg/naireland/contacts.html
Phone: (01) 672 8000

All of the above numbers are central. They will be able to advise you on your local branch. The websites will also have this and more general information. Numbers for all these organisations are also available in the coloured pages of your local telephone directory under 'personal numbers'.

Why are so few rapes reported?

- Most rapes are carried out by someone known to the victim. This prevents some victims reporting the crime.
- A medical examination is usually required within 24 hours of the rape. This can be very traumatic for the victim.
- Fear of publicity during the rape trial or of what the attacker will do when released from prison can put off many victims.
- Having to re-live the experience during the trial may be too traumatic for some victims.

  Note

  Unlike in some American states (as often portrayed in films) a woman's sexual history cannot be used as a defence in this country.

  The rape victim's name and address cannot be made public.

  Rape is a crime; it is the state, not the victim, that prosecutes the attacker. This means that the victim does not have to employ a solicitor or pay legal costs.

Many women are taking self-defence classes to learn how to protect themselves.

If you are being attacked – although the attacker may have a weapon

- Shout as loudly as you can for help.
- Kick the attacker in the shins.
- Spray perfume or deodorant in the attacker's eyes if you have these in your bag.
- Run to a public place or a house.

Common feelings after a rape attack

- Numb
- Contaminated
- Angry
- Helpless
- Depressed
- Guilty
- Afraid.

What you should do

- Do not keep it to yourself; tell someone.
- Report the attack to the Gardai.
- If you need to go to the doctor do not go alone; bring someone you trust with you for support.
- Talk to someone in a Rape Crisis Centre. They will know best how to support you.

 **ACTIVITY**

> ## Man Found Guilty of Rape
>
> An unemployed docker was found guilty today of raping his former girlfriend at an apartment once occupied by both of them in the city centre. The rape was said to be all the more harrowing as it was committed in the presence of their three-year-old daughter. Paul Owens (29), who claims that he has been having severe bouts of depression since he split up with the victim, was remanded in custody to Mountjoy Jail where he awaits sentencing on Monday.

1. Do you think it matters that the victim was once Paul Owen's girlfriend? Explain your answer.

   _____
   _____
   _____

2. Why do you think Paul Owen raped this young woman?

   _____
   _____
   _____

3. What do you think the woman should do now to help herself and her child?

   _____
   _____
   _____

Rape Crisis Services and Centres in Ireland

There are currently a total of 17 rape crisis centres in Ireland. Go to www.oneinfour.org/links/rapecrisis/ for a list of all 17 centres. The majority of centres have websites and free phone numbers.

 **ACTIVITY**

Look through local and national newspapers for reported rape cases. Discuss them in class. Take special note of the following issues:

1. Many people think rape is a crime committed by strangers. Do the articles that you have read bear this out?

2. What kind of sentences do the rapists receive in the cases you have read?
3. Is there anything else that you notice or think is important to point out after reading the articles?

Points to discuss:
- Can sex offenders be rehabilitated?
- Do you think that convicted sex offenders should be tracked by the Gardaí after finishing their prison sentence?

Unplanned Pregnancy

Shock, numbness and fear are the words often used by young women who are faced with an unplanned pregnancy. To many women who have not yet completed their education or secured a fulfilling job, an unplanned pregnancy can create a great deal of pain, indecision and confusion. Many feel totally alone. Perhaps they are not in a very secure relationship and do not know how the baby's father will take the news. Others fear the reaction of family, neighbours and friends. Some young women who have had an unplanned pregnancy report how they kept their pregnancy to themselves for a long period of time, putting off dealing with the fact for as long as possible.

Where to go for help and advice

The Irish Family Planning Association
Head Office: 60 Amiens Street, Dublin 1. Tel: (01) 806 9444. Web: www.ifpa.ie.

This organisation provides the following services to women:
- Free pregnancy test
- Free pregnancy counselling
- Information and practical advice on all the options
- Continuing with the pregnancy and keeping the baby
- Adoption and fostering
- Abortion – information about clinics in England
- Pre- and post-abortion counselling.

Telephone (01) 806 9444 and they will advise on the address and phone number of the clinic nearest you.

CURA and LIFE

Both these organisations offer the following services:

- Free pregnancy test
- Counselling
- Practical and emotional support during and after the birth of your baby
- Referral to adoption and fostering agencies if requested.

Neither of these organisations considers abortion an acceptable option in any circumstances and will therefore not provide abortion information. They do, however, offer post-abortion counselling.

CURA

Tel: Locall 1850 622626. Web: www.cura.ie

LIFE

Tel: Locall 1850 281281. Web: www.life.ie.

Both the contact numbers above are central. If you ring them, they will be able to tell you the address and telephone number of the CURA or LIFE centre nearest you.

Abortion and the law

Abortion is currently not legal in Ireland under any circumstances. However, Irish women have the right to travel to England where abortion is legal during the first 24 weeks of pregnancy if the mother's physical or mental health is at risk. Women are also entitled to information on abortion. Pre- and post-abortion counselling is advised.

ACTIVITY

Read Tom's story below and then answer the questions that follow.
I had just left college and this was my first job. The money and the prospects of promotion were good so I felt that I had really landed on my feet. Lorraine came to work in the firm on a college work placement, I fancied her the minute I saw her. After a few days I asked her to come for a drink with me after work and she did. We had a great time and talked and talked. We really seemed to have a lot in common. We continued to see each other even after she returned to college. Everything seemed perfect, our sex life was great and we really seemed to be made for each other.

Lorraine did not want to go on the pill so we used condoms as a method of contraception. On a few occasions we got a bit careless about using them. Looking back it was really irresponsible of both of us.

Lorraine told me that she was pregnant on 12 January. That date will stick in my mind for the rest of my life. She was really upset about the fact. I don't really blame her, as she was a good bit younger than me and, unlike me, had not yet finished college. From the outset my gut reaction was to keep the baby, but Lorraine didn't want to. I offered to support her and the baby financially, and told her that she could always take time out and return to college later.

Lorraine comes from a very strict family and she really feared what they would say. In the end Lorraine decided that she was going to go to England for an abortion. She felt that she was too young to have a baby. I tried to persuade her not to but she said that it was her body and her life and that she had made up her mind. I was devastated.

I even rang a solicitor to see what my rights were. I was horrified but not really surprised that I had really no rights.

Lorraine went to England on her own on 25 March and had the abortion the next day. I suppose I should have gone to support her but I could not bring myself to do so. I felt that what she was doing was wrong. When she came back, we were like strangers. She felt that I had let her down, and I felt that she had let me down. Things were never the same after that and we split up about three weeks later. That was four years ago. Even now I often wonder what might have been. What our baby would have looked like.

1. Why do you think Lorraine decided to have an abortion?

   _____
   _____
   _____

2. How do you think Lorraine felt when she went to England?

   _____
   _____
   _____

3. Do you think Tom should have gone with her? Explain your answer.

   _____
   _____
   _____

4. Do you think that fathers should have more rights? Explain your answer.

   _____
   _____
   _____

The Rights of Unmarried Fathers

One in three children in Ireland are now born to unmarried parents, yet, unlike the mother or a married man, the constitution gives unmarried fathers no automatic status in the lives of their children. Under the Guardian of Infants Act 1964 the sole guardian of a non-marital child is its mother. Until 1987, the natural father had a right to apply for custody and access but had no right to apply for joint guardianship. Nowadays, an unmarried father may become joint guardian of his children by swearing a statutory declaration. However, if the mother doesn't agree to this, the father must still apply to court to be made a guardian. Unmarried fathers must give their consent to have their name included on their child's birth certificate.

CD - Track 17

Listen to the news item on Track 17 about the 2007 landmark High Court case on the rights of unmarried fathers. Use the information you hear together with the information above to answer the questions below.

1. Why did Mr G take the mother of his children to court?

2. Mr G did not apply for joint custody of his children until after they were taken to England. Why do you think he failed to do this?

3. Usually if an unmarried father has not applied for joint custody, he has few rights. Why do you think the judge ruled in favour of Mr G even though he did not have joint custody?

4. Do you feel the judge was right to rule that the mother had acted unlawfully in this case? Explain your answer.

5. Do you feel unmarried fathers are treated fairly by the laws of this country? Explain your answer.

Child Sexual Abuse

What is meant by sexual abuse?

Child sexual abuse is a very difficult subject to approach in a classroom situation as it is possible that someone in the class has experienced it in some form. Child sexual abuse is when an adult uses his or her power or authority over a child to force or persuade him or her to take part in sexual activities. Sexual abuse ranges from fondling or petting to full vaginal or anal intercourse. Incest is when the sexual abuse is committed by a family member.

Who sexually abuses?

Although both men and women sexually abuse, the majority of abusers are male. Contrary to popular myth, most sexual abuse is committed by someone known to the child – a family member, a neighbour, someone in authority or a baby-sitter. The sexual offender often has the trust of the child and of those who care for him or her and can often appear to be very ordinary. This is very far from the truth. Child sexual abusers are very disturbed, cruel individuals. They frequently know exactly what they are doing and go to great lengths to cover it up. They are not usually psychiatrically ill. Sex offenders come from all types of background. Some have very responsible jobs and are considered upstanding members of the community. This is why in the past many child victims of sexual abuse were not believed when they reported how they were being treated.

Who is abused?

Children from all types of background, both rich and poor, are abused. It is estimated that in Ireland as many as one in eight girls and one in twelve boys are sexually abused at some time before they reach their sixteenth birthday. There is no reported difference between the numbers of children from urban or rural backgrounds being abused.

The effects of abuse

Sexual abuse affects different children in different ways, so although some general effects will be given here each child is unique, and how this terrible experience affects them will be different for each child. General effects include:

- Loss of trust in all adults.
- Poor self-esteem.
- Extreme nervousness or panic attacks.
- Feelings of guilt, as some children convince themselves that they are in some way responsible for what has happened to them.
- Shame.

As the child moves into adulthood, they may have difficulty forming lasting sexual relationships. Because of low self-esteem they may get into abusive relationships, believing themselves to be undeserving of anything better. A person who has been abused as a child may go to sexual extremes, either being unable to have any sexual relationships or behaving very promiscuously. In an attempt to forget what has happened some may resort to alcohol or other drugs. However, with skilled help, victims of child sexual abuse can move on to a new and satisfying life.

What help is available for victims of sexual abuse?

If you have been sexually abused yourself, or know someone who has been sexually abused in the past, there are organisations that can try to help. It is important to remember that because someone has been sexually abused does not mean that they will automatically develop permanent emotional problems.

The 17 Rape Crisis Centres around the country provide help for both male and female adults who have been sexually abused as children. Their addresses and phone numbers are available at www.oneinfour.org/links/rapecrisis/

Eating Disorders

The three common eating disorders are food addiction, anorexia and bulimia. All three can have very serious consequences for health and will be considered briefly here. Suggestions for further research will be offered after each section.

Food addiction

Sufferers go through periods of binge eating in order to cope with emotional and psychological problems. Usually there is excessive weight gain. (See the article in Exam Time, below.)

Anorexia nervosa

This is an eating disorder characterised by the deliberate refusal to eat enough to maintain a normal body weight. As a result, both the body and the mind are starved of the nutrients needed to function as normal. The condition is most common in girls and women aged 10 to 30 years old (90 per cent of sufferers are female). Sufferers are unable to see that anorexia is a serious illness which can be fatal. Full recovery is possible with appropriate support and treatment.

People suffering from anorexia are unable to discriminate between normal and abnormal body weight

If you are interested in finding out more about this condition the website www.bodywhys.ie provides a great deal of information on anorexia and the help and support options that are available.

Bulimia nervosa

This disorder is characterised by repeated episodes of binge eating followed by behaviour aimed at compensating for this out-of-control eating – fasting, making oneself vomit, using laxatives and diuretics or appetite suppressants (slimming tablets), and excessive exercising. In many cases, bulimia begins with a diet but the preoccupation with food and weight becomes obsessive and can take over the person's life. Eventually, they will become locked into a cycle of bingeing and purging (getting rid of the food) or resorting to other ways of preventing weight gain.

People suffering from bulimia are often of normal weight but frequently have other health problems, e.g. digestive problems, poor skin, headaches, mouth ulcers, rotting teeth and irregular periods. If you are interested in finding out more about this condition the website www.bodywhys.ie provides a great deal of information on bulimia and the help and support options that are available.

 **KEY ASSIGNMENT**

For this key assignment you should write out on a sheet of paper a list of the agencies or organisations that help with health or addiction problems. List the address and phone number of each and explain the services they provide.

Some of the agencies you might like to include are: Irish Family Planning Association, Alcoholics Anonymous, CURA, Rape Crisis Centre, Childline, LIFE, Narcotics Anonymous, Aware, Al-Anon, Al-Teen, the Samaritans. Keep this key assignment in your Social Education folder as evidence of completion.

When you have completed this key assignment, go to page 147 and tick off Assignment 4 on the checklist.

📄 EXAM TIME

Social Education (2005) – short question

1. If a couple are not married, the father must give his consent before his name is placed on the child's birth certificate.   True ☐   False ☐

Social Education (2005) – long question (part)

2.

> **The Little Box of Domestic Horrors**
> Rape
> House slave
> Constant criticism
> Terror
> Frightened children
> Silence
> Beating
> Shouting

   (a) Domestic abuse can be categorised into three main types: sexual, physical and psychological. Which do you think is the worst type of abuse? Explain why.
   Type: _____
   Explain: _____
   _____

   (b) What advice would you give to a woman living in an abusive situation?
   _____
   _____

   (c) Name an organisation/agency that works with victims of domestic abuse.
   _____

Social Education (2006) – short question

3. A father has automatic guardianship rights in respect of his child if his name is on the child's birth certificate.   True ☐   False ☐

Social Education (2006) – long question (part)

4. Domestic Abuse: The facts

   (a) 'According to this research one in seven women and one in sixteen men have been subjected to severe abusive behaviour by a partner.'
   Look at the bar chart on the opposite page. What percentage of women and what percentage of men have experienced **severe abuse of any type?**

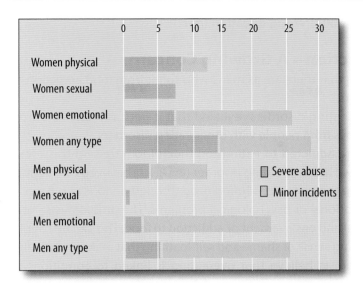

Women: _____   Men: _____

(b)   'About half of those experiencing severe abuse were physically injured but only a
       minority reported the abuse.'
       Why do you think so few reported the abuse?

       _____

       _____

       _____

(c)   'Those at highest risk of experiencing severe abuse included young people, those
       who have little control over domestic finances and those with weak links to family
       or community.'
       Select **one** of the groups listed above and explain why you think members of this
       group are more likely to become victims of domestic abuse.
       Group: _____
       Explain:_____

       _____

(d)   'According to the ESRI report 26 per cent of men experienced either minor or
       severe abuse.'
       Does this finding surprise you? Explain your answer.

       _____

       _____

(e)   Mention **two** things that the government could do to address the issue of
       domestic violence.
       1. _____
       2. _____

Social Education (2007) – long question (part)

Food Addiction – A Growing Concern

It now appears that there are as many who suffer from food addiction as other eating disorders.

A helpline for eating disorders revealed that it gets as many calls from food addicts as it does from people with other eating disorders.

People who are addicted to eating too much food are said to suffer from a condition known as binge eating disorder (BED). It is believed that as many men as women have this condition. Sufferers go through periods of binge eating to cope with emotional or psychological problems. The problem is so great that many often feel and enslavement or addiction to food. This can be coupled with an overwhelming sense of shame and self-loathing that makes it difficult to seek help. Psychologists believe that overeating is linked to conditions such as depression and that some sufferers use food as a means of suppressing negative feelings about themselves and their past experiences.

5. (a) What is binge eating disorder (BED)?

_____

_____

(b) Why, according to the article, do people binge eat?

_____

_____

(c) Why is it difficult for binge eaters to seek help?

_____

_____

(d) Name and describe **one** other eating disorder.

Name: _____

Description: _____

_____

_____

Social Education (2008) – long question (part)

6. Select **one** of the organisations above.

Name of organisation: _____

(a) Name and describe the specific group that this organisation helps.

_____
_____

(b) Describe the main service provided by this organisation.

_____
_____

Module FIVE

Contemporary Issues 2

This module should be completed during session 3 (Year 2).

Below are seven key assignments for this module. You should choose FOUR of these. One of them must be a group activity and one must be an out-of-school activity. As you work through the module and do your chosen assignments, come back to this page and tick off each of them.

1. I took part in a debate on a contemporary issue.

    Date: ___ / ___ / _____

2. I examined a contemporary issue with a group of students in my class. Then each one of us presented this issue in a different format: as a short report, press release, news broadcast, image, article for a school magazine, collage or illustrated fact sheet.

    Date: ___ / ___ / _____

3. I wrote to my local newspaper or political representative about an issue of interest to me.

    OR:

    I presented an illustrated fact sheet about a contemporary issue.

    Date: ___ / ___ / _____

4. I tracked an issue in a newspaper or on television for three days and gave a brief report to my class about it.

    OR:

    I created a two-minute slot for a radio programme in support of a local issue.

    Date: ___ / ___ / _____

5. I gave a brief report to my class about crime in my local area.

    Date: ___ / ___ / _____

6. I took part with others in a roleplay about my civil rights.

    Date: ___ / ___ / _____

7. I collected a registration form, filled it in and posted it off to register my name on the Register of Electors.

    Date: ___ / ___ / _____

UNIT 1 Influences on Contemporary Issues: The Media

In this unit you will be looking at various contemporary issues in terms of how different factors, such as media sensationalism and bias, can affect our thoughts and opinions about these issues.

 ACTIVITY

Media Survey

1. Which of these media forms would be generally available to you at home?

    TV   Radio   CDs/tapes   Video

    Internet   Magazines   Newspapers   Journals

2. Which of the above would you use most?

    1. _____   2. _____   3. _____

3. Have you watched the news in the past week?   Yes   No

4. Have you read a newspaper in the past week?   Yes   No

    If yes, which one(s)? _____

5. Do you watch documentaries regularly?   Yes   No

    If yes, what was the last one you watched? _____

6. Do you use the Internet regularly?   Yes   No

    If yes, what do you generally use it for? _____

Young People and Contemporary Issues

ACTIVITY

Some issues are of more concern to young people than others. In your group, brainstorm as many of these issues as you can think of. From this list pick the eight most popular ones among your group. Record these below.

Issues of concern to young people

As a group, over a period of time gather local and national newspapers. Try to have a mixture of both tabloid (e.g. the *Star*) and broadsheet (e.g. the *Independent*) newspapers. Examine the newspapers for articles about each of the issues recorded above. Cut out all the relevant articles and display them. As a group read through them, paying particular attention to the points below:

- How many of the issues were reported on?
- Were the issues dealt with in detail?
- Were photographs or captions included?
- Were the issues given an important place in the papers, e.g. on the front page?
- What was the paper's tone/attitude to the issues?
- How were young people portrayed in the articles?

You could also use RTÉ's website – go to www.rte.ie and click on 'news'. This website has an archive section, which could be very useful for tracking issues of interest.

🔑 KEY ASSIGNMENT

For this key assignment your class must divide up into groups of approximately six students. Each group should pick a contemporary issue of interest to them. These issues must be examined in detail, with each group member then reporting on the issue using a different format: as a short report, press release, news broadcast, image, article for a school magazine, collage or illustrated fact sheet.

When you have completed this key assignment, go to page 197 and tick off Assignment 2 on the checklist.

Example: Press release

Date: *This is the date you send the press release to the paper.*

Embargo: *You are telling the paper not to publish the details of the press release before this date; if there is no embargo you write 'none'.*

Contact: *Name of the person sending the press release to the paper.*

Huge Shopping Complex to Put *Give your press release a clear heading*
Small Businesses in Jeopardy

Navan Chamber of Commerce warned today that if the proposed mega shopping complex on the Dublin road were to go ahead it would spell disaster for small businesses in the town.

Those in favour of the complex claimed that it would pose no threat to existing traders. Councillor James Ryan, who is in favour of the complex, claimed that, 'because the population of Navan is growing so rapidly there is enough business for everyone'.

Local traders are planning a protest march to the county council offices on Friday next.

 Press releases need to be precise and to the points giving all the relevant details. You can include quotes from people involved in the issue. Type up using double spacing.

Ends:  *Write 'ends' so that the editor knows the article is finished.*

CD - Track 18

Example: News broadcast
The person who chooses this format will have to come up with a story and then write out a script for it. They will then have to tape record themselves delivering the broadcast. Listen to the sample news broadcast on Track 18 and answer the questions.

1. Why is the Catholic church described as a 'burden' in this article?
   _____
   _____
   _____

2. What did the minister say about anti-Aids funding? _____
   _____
   _____

3. What is your opinion of the Catholic Church's opposition to contraception?
   _____
   _____
   _____

How Events Become Issues

Sometimes one particular event, because it gets publicity, can trigger a debate and in this way become an issue. Take the following examples. Write down what issues these events raise.

Three young boys lose their lives when 14-year-old David Hawks opens fire on his classmates in a New York high school.

Issue(s) _____
_____

A well-known Dublin solicitor is given four years for the killing of Laura Jones in a drink-driving accident two years ago. Laura's family is horrified by the light sentence.

Issue(s) _____
_____

A 12-year-old boy is driven to suicide by classmates' cruelty.

Issue(s) _____
_____

The mother of four-year-old Suzanne Roe, who weighs almost seven stone, fears that her daughter could die without urgent medical attention.

Issue(s) _____
_____

CD - Track 19

Listen to the debate on Track 19, and then answer the questions.

1. What is the motion for this debate?

_____

2. What are the main points put forward for the motion?

_____

_____

_____

3. What are the main points put forward against the motion?

_____

_____

_____

_____

4. How did both speakers try to make the debate more interesting?

_____

_____

_____

_____

5. If you were debating this issue, would you be for or against the motion? Explain your answer.

                       For   Against

Reason _____

_____

_____

KEY ASSIGNMENT

For this key assignment you must take part in a debate about a contemporary issue.
When you have completed this key assignment, go to page 197 and tick off Assignment 1 on the checklist.

Possible motions

Irish people should be very sympathetic to the cause of refugees and asylum seekers.

There is no excuse for the unemployed.

A student's life is an easy one.

Cannabis should not be made legal.

Divorce is not a good idea.

Drugs should be allowed in sport.

Add some motions of your own.

_____

_____

_____

Contemporary Issues and the Media

Usually the way we learn of contemporary issues is through the media. Generally it is only issues very local to us, for example issues concerning people in our parish or our town, that we learn about first hand. The media, therefore, has a very big influence on how various issues are presented and on how public opinion is formed. Sensationalism and bias are two characteristics of the media that can sometimes distort or colour our understanding of various contemporary issues.

ACTIVITY

Look up the words 'sensationalism' and 'bias' in a dictionary and write down what you find below.

Sensationalism

_____

_____

Bias

_____

_____

Ask Us before You Judge Us

If you believe the media, teenage life is all about drink, drugs and sex. But a new campaign calls for more mature coverage, explain Maria Kelly and Stephanie Kelly

'The G-string round your ankle if you're up for sex.' Have we got your attention yet? When journalists splash headings like this across the front page of newspapers, that's what they are trying to do: shock readers at the expense of young people. And at a Dáil na nÓg council meeting last June teenagers gathered to discuss the effects of these appalling tactics.

One of the main recommendations from this meeting was that the media urgently need to amend the way it portrays teenagers and start giving us a say in how these issues are covered. From this meeting the Fairsay campaign was formed and this article marks the launch of this campaign.

However strongly we felt, we knew adults wouldn't take our word for it, so we decided to back up our claims with research. Many of the delegates at Dáil na nÓg 2007 believed teenagers were negatively portrayed in the media coverage of the Junior Cert celebrations, and this period was made the focus of our main research. For a week before the Junior Cert results day, and a week after, we monitored every national and local newspaper in Ireland, with the help of media monitoring experts.

The first thing we noticed was the difference of approach taken by broadsheet newspapers as compared to tabloids. Broadsheets portray teenagers in a better light, concentrating more on positive aspects of the Junior Cert results day. In fact, one of the most positive articles that we found – 'we don't need to drink to have fun' – was in the *Sunday Independent* and a very similar article which appeared in *The Irish Times* – 'I don't need to drink for a good night out' – also got the Fairsay stamp of approval.

We should also tell you that the broadsheets weren't all on our side, with many articles giving far too much space to the issue of underage drinking. This confirmed for us the media's obsession with teenagers who binge drink as opposed to teenagers who don't drink, or drink in moderation.

Tabloids, on the other hand, were more provocative in their reports of Junior Cert celebrations. We found their headlines to be over-the-top, and worded purely for shock value. Headlines like 'the G-string round your ankle if you're up for sex' are obviously going to attract attention.

We were disgusted to read stories about sexual promiscuity on Junior Cert night which contained lewd descriptions, hearsay and innuendo. It was noted that female students were treated more unfairly then male students in this context.

Sex wasn't the only hot topic. Along with the broadsheets, tabloid newspapers appear to be obsessed with underage drinking and drug use. One particular tabloid article that stood out was the story whose headline alone caused a stir – 'Straight Es' was labelled as one of the most sensationalist articles by Fairsay. The article recounted how three young girls went to a dealer to buy Ecstasy to help celebrate their results. The article quoted what we would question was a reliable source.

We in the Fairsay campaign are realists. We know the print and broadcast media have a duty to report that some young people choose to spend their Junior Certificate results night drinking and behaving in an irresponsible manner. But we believe that these young people are in the minority and we question whether it is right to take advantage of young people who don't celebrate wisely.

So what do we want? We want a voice. We want to be heard. We want print journalists, television and radio presenters and editors to get into contact with us about the Fairsay campaign so they can hear what we have to say. We are tired of listening to adults talking, often negatively, about teenagers. We want to be talked to, not just talked about. We want an end to the media negativity that is creating a false portrayal of Irish teenagers today.

The Irish Times, 14 December 2007

ACTIVITY

1. Name **two** tabloid and **two** broadsheet newspapers being sold in Ireland today.
   Tabloid
   1. _____
   2. _____
   Broadsheet
   1. _____
   2. _____
   Which of these types of newspaper does the Fairplay campaign believe uses sensationalism and bias most?
   _____

2. What is the main aim of the Fairsay campaign?
   _____
   _____

3. Fairsay believes that the media frequently represent young people unfairly. How and why do they believe the media do this?
   _____
   _____
   _____

4. If someone came to earth from another planet, how would they think young people behave if all they had to go on was what is reported in the media?

    _____

    _____

    _____

5. Examine the newspapers and watch television reports around the time the Junior Certificate results come out in mid-September. If you miss this time of year you can view news archives on www.rte.ie. What stories are making the headlines? Do you think they accurately represent young people?

    _____

    _____

    _____

🔍 KEY ASSIGNMENT

For this key assignment you are required to track or follow an issue on TV or in the newspapers for three days. You must then report to the class about the issue.

When you have completed this key assignment, go to page 197 and tick off Assignment 4 on the checklist.

Issue tracking

What issue are you tracking? _____

Are you tracking the issue through the papers?

                    Yes   No

If so, which paper(s) are you using?

_____

_____

Are you tracking the issue through the news?

                    Yes   No

If so, which station(s) are you watching/listening to?

_____

_____

Day 1

Date _____

What were the main points made by the broadcast/article?

_____

_____

_____

Day 2

Date _____

What were the main points made by the broadcast/article?

_____

_____

_____

Day 3

Date _____

What were the main points made by the broadcast/article?

_____

_____

_____

CD - Track 20

Listen to Track 20. On it an LCA student interviews a member of a local action group about a local issue. This interview is an example of a two-minute radio programme slot. Answer the questions that follow.

1. What issue is being addressed in the interview?

    _____

    _____

2. What action group does Cathy represent?

    _____

    _____

3. What are the main concerns of this action group?

    _____

    _____

4. What information do they base their concerns on?

_____

_____

_____

5. What is Cathy's group doing to help the issue?

_____

_____

_____

 KEY ASSIGNMENT

For this key assignment you are required to create a two-minute slot for a radio programme in support of a local issue.

When you have completed this key assignment, go to page 197 and tick off Assignment 4 on the checklist.

EXAM TIME

Social Education (2008) – long question (part)

1. Do you agree or disagree with this statement?

    Agree   ▢   Disagree   ▢   (tick your choice)

    Explain your answer:

    _____

    _____

2. Name **one** contemporary issue that you studied in detail. _____

    (a) Why is this issue a concern for society?

    _____

    _____

    (b) Name a voluntary organisation that positively affects the selected issue.

    _____

UNIT 2 Influences on Contemporary Issues: Interest Groups

Interest groups exist for one of two reasons:

- To promote the interests of their members, e.g. Irish Farmers' Association.
- To promote a cause for the common good, e.g. Greenpeace works for the preservation of the earth's environment.

When an interest group tries to make changes at government level on an issue of importance, the interest group sometimes becomes called a 'pressure group'. Pressure groups try to make changes in some or all of the following ways:

Lobbying   Putting pressure on politicians.

Campaigning   Getting public interest by organising different events, advertising campaigns, etc.

Awareness raising   Putting together information programmes and leaflets.

Non-violent action   Marches, protests, strikes, boycotts.

The main aims of these actions are usually one and sometimes all of the following:

- To improve a service.
- To change government policy.
- To change public attitudes/behaviour.
- To protect human rights.
- To prevent a disaster.

1. What message is this poster trying to get across?

    _____

    _____

    _____

2. Do you think that this poster is effective?

    Yes ☐   No ☐

Have you ever **felt afraid** of someone who is close to you?

If you or someone you know is experiencing domestic violence, **Women's Aid** can help.

Women's Aid Freephone Helpline

1800 341 900

Explain your answer.

_____

_____

_____

KEY ASSIGNMENT

For this key assignment you must:

A. Write a letter to your local newspaper or political representative about an issue of importance to you.

OR:

B. Present an illustrated fact sheet about an issue of importance to you.

Keep a copy of your letter/fact sheet in your Social Education folder as evidence of assignment completion.

When you have completed this key assignment, go to page 197 and tick off Assignment 3 on the checklist.

KEY ASSIGNMENT

For this key assignment you must give a brief report to your class about crime in your area. Below are some ideas as to where you can get information for your report.

When you have completed this key assignment, go to page 197 and tick off Assignment 5 on the checklist.

ACTIVITY

Below is a list of interest groups. Most have websites. Find out:
A.   What are the main aim(s) of each group.
B.   What contemporary issue(s) is each group concerned about.
C.   How they try to make changes concerning the issue(s) of importance to them.

Find out the same information about one or two local interest groups campaigning in your area. Keep the information you find out in your Social Education folder. It may be of use when you do your contemporary issue task.

Interest groups

ISPCC	ISPCA
Trocaire	ICA
IFA	Amnesty International
Greenpeace	Focus Ireland
Oxfam	Barnardo's
Pavee Point	ICA
IFA	INOU (unemployed)
Irish Wheelchair Association	Irish Refugee Council
National Youth Council of Ireland	Women's Aid

Rogge calls for Tibet resolution

The president of the International Olympic Committee, Jacques Rogge, has called for a 'rapid peaceful resolution in Tibet' following protests along the torch's relay route in London on Sunday.

Demonstrators, many of them challenging China's policies in Tibet and Darfur, tried to board a torch relay bus and also attempted to grab the torch during the procession. One protester tried to snuff out the flame with what appeared to be a fire extinguisher.

Speaking in Beijing today, Rogge confirmed the IOC's 'serious concern' for the situation in Tibet in his strongest comments to date on the growing political unrest surrounding the 2008 Games.

'I'm very concerned with the international situation and what's happening in Tibet,' he said.

'The torch relay has been targeted. The International Olympic Committee has expressed its serious concern and calls for a rapid peaceful resolution in Tibet.'

RTÉ News 7 April 2008

Why are demonstrators protesting against China's occupation of Tibet?

China's military invaded Tibet in 1949 and took over. China feels that it has a historical right to rule Tibet because of agreements made hundreds of years ago between Tibetan and Chinese leaders. China contends that Tibet is actually part of China and that they are in fact liberating the Tibetan people. Some sections of Tibetan society, however, strongly disagree with this view and want independence from China with the Dalai Lama as their leader. International objection (e.g. by the United Nations) to China's occupation of Tibet centres on how China is enforcing its rule.

Protests against China's human rights violations in Tibet

It is estimated that since 1949 at least 1.2 million Tibetans have died as a direct result of the Chinese invasion and occupation. China opened prisons and forced labour camps all over Tibet where they sent Tibetans who spoke out against them. Conditions in these prisons and camps were reported to be horrific – torture, forced labour, starvation and abuse were believed to be commonplace. Some reports state that up until very recently 70 per cent of all those incarcerated in Tibetan prisons died. Other reports claim that the Chinese authorities actually shot prisoners in groups of ten or twenty to keep the prison population down to levels they could control. China has been very careful not to allow the international community know the extent of what has gone on in Tibet. The Chinese government has done this by releasing pro-Chinese propaganda, limiting the movement of Tibetan people throughout and outside the country and by limiting access to the country by the international media.

Throughout the years Tibetan activists have staged demonstrations against the Chinese regime. These demonstrations have frequently resulted in mass killings and arrests. Grounds for arrest and imprisonment seem to be found in any kind of activity: Tibetans have been arrested for speaking with foreigners, or singing patriotic songs, or putting up posters, or possessing copies of an autobiography of the Dalai Lama or some video or audio cassette about him, or for wearing traditional Tibetan clothes on Chinese national day.

Reports of torture are plentiful. Methods and instruments of torture and ill-treatment have been described by a number of former prisoners who had been subjected to them. These include indiscriminate beating with anything available, such as electric batons, kicking, punching, hitting with rifle-butts, sticks, and even iron bars. In prison, cruel and degrading methods of torture for the purpose of extracting confessions have been reported. These include setting guard dogs on prisoners, using electric batons, especially on women prisoners in extremely perverted and degrading ways, inflicting cigarette burns and administering electric shocks.

1. Why did the protestors try to extinguish the Olympic torch before the 2008 summer Olympics in Beijing?

   _____

   _____

2. Why does China feel it has the right to rule Tibet?

   _____

   _____

3. Do all the Tibetan people agree with this? Explain your answer.

   _____

   _____

   _____

   _____

4. The United Nations has consistently criticised China over its human rights record in Tibet. From this article can you list **four** human rights that are being violated in Tibet? (See UN Declaration of Human Rights in Module 3.)

   (a) _____

   (b) _____

   (c) _____

   (d) _____

5. What do you think can be done by the international community to force China to improve its human rights record in Tibet?

   _____

   _____

   _____

   _____

6. Some people feel that China has kept the world in the dark about Tibet. How, is it believed, have they managed to do this?

   _____

   _____

   _____

 **EXAM TIME**

Social Education (2006) – short question
Select one of the organisations below and explain in detail the work that it does.

Organisation: _____

Explain: _____

_____

_____

UNIT 3 Democratic Institutions

Local Government

Local government, sometimes called the local authority, takes care of the day-to-day business of your local area. The local authority is under the supervision of the Ministry for the Environment and is made up of two parts:

- Elected members
- Full-time manager

The name of your local authority will depend on the type of area you live in. Your local authority may be called any one of the following:

- Borough council
- Town commission
- County borough council
- Urban district council
- County council

How local authorities are elected

Local elections are usually held every five years. Every person who is 18 years of age or older on 15 April in the year of the elections and living in the area is entitled to a vote. If you want to check

Right to life of the unborn	1983
Voting right at Dáil	1984
Single European Act	1987
Right to travel	1992
Right to information	1992
Divorce	1995
Bail	1996
Cabinet confidentiality	1997
Amsterdam Treaty	1998
Northern Ireland Peace Treaty	1998
Local government	1999
Death penalty	2001
International Criminal Court	2001
Nice Treaty	2001
Abortion	2002
Citizenship	2004
Lisbon Treaty	2008
Child protection	(proposed)

ACTIVITY

Pick an issue and hold your own referendum in class. Use the sample referendum paper above as a guide.

As we saw above, the Oireachtas or Irish parliament is made up of three parts – the President, the Dáil and the Seanad. Each of these will now be looked at in turn.

The President

The office of President is the highest in the land. Presidential elections are held every seven years (unless a President dies in office) and a President can serve for two terms, which would be a total of 14 years. In order to stand in a presidential election you must be at least 35 years old. Every citizen of Ireland over the age of 18 is entitled to vote in presidential elections.

Mary McAleese

ACTIVITY

Who is our current President? _____

Compile a profile of the President. Try to include a photograph and as much information as you can find out about him/her.

The role of the President

The main role that the President has in this country concerns issues related to the constitution. In recent times, though, the office of President has become a very public one and the President often represents Ireland abroad.

Past presidents of Ireland

Douglas Hyde	1938–1945
Sean T O'Kelly	1945–1959
Éamon de Valera	1959–1973
Erskine Childers	1973–1974
Cearbhall O'Dalaigh	1974–1976
Patrick Hillery	1976–1990
Mary Robinson	1990–1997
Mary McAleese	1997–

Others since this book was printed

_____

_____

The Dáil – TDs

There are 166 seats in total in the Dáil. After an election these seats are filled by TDs (or Teachta Dála) from all over the country. TDs can be members of the various political parties in the country or, if they are not members of any political party, they are independent TDs. The main political parties in Ireland today are Fianna Fáil, Fine Gael, Sinn Féin, Labour and the Green Party. After an election the political party (or combination of several political parties) that wins the most seats form the government. TDs who have been elected but are not in the government party/parties form the opposition.

The Government

The Government consists of between 7 and 15 people. This group of people must include:

- The Taoiseach (Prime Minister)
- The Tánaiste (Deputy Prime Minister)
- The Minister for Finance

There are also a number of other ministers who take particular responsibility for various government departments. Government ministers are also called cabinet members.

⚙ ACTIVITY

What political parties are currently in government? _____

What political parties are currently in opposition? _____

_____

Who is the current leader of:

Fianna Fáil? _____

Fine Gael? _____

Sinn Féin? _____

The Labour Party? _____

The Green Party? _____

Who is the current Taoiseach? _____

Who is the current Tánaiste? _____

Below is a list of ministerial positions. Find out who is currently the holder of each.

Finance _____

Health and children _____

Enterprise, trade and employment _____

Transport _____

Justice equality and law reform _____

Foreign affairs _____

Arts, sports and tourism _____

Community, rural and Gaeltacht affairs _____

Social and family affairs _____

Defence _____

Environment, heritage and local government _____

Communications _____

Agriculture, fisheries and food _____

Education and science _____

This information is available on the government website www.taoiseach.gov.ie/. (On the home page click on 'Taoiseach and Government' and then on 'List of Ministers'.)

Create posters with pictures of the current Taoiseach, Tánaiste, government ministers and MEPs on them. Hang them up around the classroom – this will help you remember who they are. You are nearly always asked to name certain politicians in your written exam.

The Seanad
The Seanad comprises 60 senators and it also sits in Leinster House. The main function of the Seanad is to advise the Dáil.

European Representation
Ireland joined the European Community (EC) in 1973. Other countries have joined since then and the EC continues to grow, with new countries applying to join every year. The idea behind the EC is that there is strength in numbers. This means both economic strength and military strength. There are three main institutions or bodies that make up the European Community or Union. These are:
- The European Parliament
- The European Commission
- The European Council.

The European Parliament
The European Parliament currently (in 2008) has 785 members (called MEPs), of whom 13 are from Ireland. Elections are held every five years. This may change in the future. The European Parliament is much like the government of any country. It has various departments that deal with the day-to-day running of the European community.

Currently (2008) there are 27 countries in the European Union. There are other countries working towards becoming members, e.g. Turkey. In alphabetical order the members of the EU are:

- Austria
- Belgium
- Bulgaria
- Cyprus
- Czech Republic
- Denmark
- Estonia
- Finland
- France
- Germany
- Greece
- Hungary
- Ireland
- Italy
- Latvia
- Lithuania
- Luxembourg
- Malta
- Netherlands
- Poland
- Portugal
- Romania
- Slovakia
- Slovenia
- Spain
- Sweden
- United Kingdom.

Name an MEP who has been elected to the European Parliament from your constituency or a constituency near you:

_____

Who is the current President of the EU? _____

The European Commission

The European Commission mainly concerns itself with the EU budget and making sure that members of the EU uphold the laws of the union.

Ireland usually has one European Commissioner. Can you name him or her?

_____

The European Council

Ministers from all the member states, together with heads of national governments (the Taoiseach in Ireland's case), meet to discuss various issues concerning the EU and its member states. Which ministers are called to the council depends on the nature of the matter that has arisen: for example, the movement of beef throughout the EU would concern our Minister for Agriculture and Food and she or he would go along to represent Ireland's views at the council meeting.

⚙ ACTIVITY

1. What is the constitution?

   _____

   _____

2. The Oireachtas or the Irish Parliament is made up of three parts. Can you name them?

   _____

   _____

3. How many TDs sit in Dáil Éireann at any one time? _____

4. What are independent TDs? _____

5. What is meant by the 'opposition party'? _____

6. In what way is Europe becoming like one big country?

    _____

    _____

    _____

📑 EXAM TIME

Social Education (2005) – short question
1. The houses of the Oireachtas are:

The Seanad and the Dáil

The House of Lords and the House of Commons

The Senate and the Council of Ministers

Social Education (2005) – long question (part)
2. (a) Select **two** of these political parties and in the case of each state the name of its leader.

Political Party _____

Leader _____

Political Party _____

Leader _____

(b) Link the Government department to the responsibility as shown in the example provided.

Government Department
a. Education
b. Defence
c. Finance
d. Environment and local government

Responsibility
1. Elections
2. Taxation
3. Schools
4. Army

a = _____3_____ ,   b = _____ ,

c = _____ ,   d = _____

Social Education (2006) – short questions

3. The current constitution of Ireland is called:

Phoblacht na hÉireann ☐

Saorstát Éireann ☐

Bunreacht na hÉireann ☐

225

4. Select the group of countries which includes all EU member states

Turkey	Estonia	Spain
Spain	Poland	Lithuania
Ireland	Malta	Switzerland

5. In order to become President of Ireland a person must be over:

25 years old   30 years old   35 years old

Social Education (2008) – short question

6. The official residence of the President of Ireland is:

The Mansion House   Áras an Uachtaráin   Dáil Eireann

UNIT 4   Active Citizenship: Voting/The Budget

Elections

There are five different kinds of election in this country. These are as follows:

Local elections
These are elections to the local authorities. Elections are usually held every five years. Elected people are called county councillors or town commissioners.

By-elections
These are held when a TD dies or resigns and his or her seat becomes vacant. An election is then held in his or her constituency to fill the vacant seat.

General elections
These are national elections held to elect the Dáil, and are held at least once every five years.

Presidential elections
These are held every seven years to elect the President (unless

the President decides to stay for a second term and nobody else comes forward).

European elections These are held every five years to elect people to represent us in Europe (MEPs).

In addition to these five elections people are also asked to vote in referenda. Referenda occur when there is a proposal to change the constitution.

Register of Electors

This is a list of all the people registered to vote in elections. A new Register of Electors is compiled and published by the local authority each year. New people are added to it, including those who have reached the age of 18, and people who have legally come to live in this country.

Anyone can look at the register. It can be inspected at any of the following locations:
- Local authority offices
- The county registrar's office
- Public libraries
- Post offices
- Garda stations.

An individual can check whether they are on the register in a particular location by looking at the website www.checktheregister.ie.

 KEY ASSIGNMENT

For this key assignment you must register to vote. As you approach your eighteenth birthday you should fill out a registration form. These can be downloaded and printed from the website www.registertovote.ie, or you could collect a form from your local post office or county council/corporation office. Some local authorities have the facility on their websites for you to register to vote online. Keep a copy of your completed registration form as evidence that you have completed this assignment.

When you have completed this assignment go to page 197 and tick off Assignment 7 on the checklist.

ACTIVITY

Have your own class election. This will help you see how a real election works.

A simulated election

1. Compile the Register of Electors.
    To do this you will have to list the full name, address and age of everyone in your class. This list will be your Register of Electors. Put a number beside each person's name.

2. Fill in polling cards.
    Some time before an election a polling card is posted to each person named in the Register of Electors. On the day of the election voters should bring this polling card together with a form of identification to their polling station. Fill out the sample below.

Polling information card

Your name and address

_____

_____

_____

Your number on the Register of Electors _____

The name of your polling station

_____

---

3. Compile a list of candidates and design a sample ballot paper.

Below is a list of five candidates on a sample ballot paper. In this election imagine there are three seats to be filled. This means that three candidates will be elected and two will not. The question is – which three? Notice that the candidates are listed in alphabetical order. On the ballot paper you mark your first preference 1, your second 2 and so on. For this ballot paper to be considered valid, it would have to be franked or stamped at the polling station.

 **CD - Track 21**

Before you vote, listen to each of the candidates telling you what their views are and what they would do if elected. (Please note that all the 'politicians', parties and party policies depicted here are fictitious.)

Mark order of preferences below	
	CARROLL (Workers' Party) LUKE CARROLL, of 66 Beachwood Drive, Glasnevin, Dublin 9 (Trade Union Official)
	DOLAN (Liberal Party) JANE DOLAN, of 18 O'Brien Ave, Drumcondra, Dublin 9 (Bank Official)
	O'BRIEN (Conservative Party) SHANE O'BRIEN, of 12 Congress Ave, Ringsend, Dublin 4 (GP)
	MACKIN (Democratic Party) BERNADETTE MACKIN, of 106 Orchard Ave, Fairview, Dublin 3 (Nurse)
	RICE (Environmental Party) KEVIN RICE, of 98 Beechwood Ave, Coolock, Dublin 5 (Lecturer)

(This page may be photocopied and used in your simulated election.)

4. Set up a simulated polling station, complete with a presiding officer (who oversees voting), a personation agent (who tries to prevent electoral offences, e.g. voting in someone else's name) and a secret ballot box to put the ballot papers in.

5. Everyone in your class should vote and place their ballot paper in the box. Do this without letting anyone else see who you voted for. This is called voting by secret ballot and means that you can vote for whoever you like and no one can put you under any pressure to vote one way or another.

Counting votes

In Ireland the system of counting votes is more complex than in some other countries, for example Britain, where you vote for only one person and do not give second preference and third preference votes, etc. The system that operates in Ireland is called 'proportional representation'. It is basically as follows:

1.   Spoiled or invalid votes are removed.

2.   First preference votes are counted for each candidate.

3.   A quota is calculated and if a candidate gets more votes than this quota in first preferences they are deemed elected.

How the quota is calculated

The quota is calculated by dividing the number of valid ballot papers (total poll minus spoiled votes) by one more than the number of seats in the constituency and adding one to the result. For example, in your election there are 28 people voting and there are three seats to be filled. The quota would be calculated thus:

$$\left(\frac{28}{3+1}\right) + 1 = 8$$

4.   The elected candidate's extra votes are divided up among the other candidates according to what the second preference is on these. If there is no second preference indicated on the papers, they are put aside.

5.   Counting goes on like this until all the seats are filled.

In the case of the presidential elections there is only one seat to be filled, that of the office of President. In this case the first person to reach the quota becomes President. The returning officer declares the results of the election.

Which three candidates did your class elect?
Name of candidate

_____

_____

_____

Social Education (2008) – short question

4. 'ALL IRISH CITIZENS OVER THE AGE OF 18 AND REGISTERED TO VOTE ARE ENTITLED TO VOTE IN THE GENERAL ELECTION'

    Why is it important for people to vote in a General Election?

    _____

    _____

UNIT 5 Civil Rights and Responsibilities

Understanding the Law

The law in Ireland can be broadly classified under four different headings:

Statute law

This branch of the law contains what are called acts. As detailed in the previous section, bills become acts if they are passed by the Dáil, the Seanad and the President. An example of an act is the Intoxicating Liquor Act 1988. This act prohibits the sale of alcohol to anyone under the age of 18, and the buying of alcohol for someone under 18.

Case law

When a case comes to the High or Supreme Court, the judge makes a decision on it based on similar cases which have occurred in the past.

Constitutional law

The constitution of this country was drawn up in 1937. It is a list of rights, responsibilities and social principles. An example of a right would be the right to a fair trial, a responsibility would be to respect your neighbour, a social principle would be that the state promises to support the institution of the family.

Common law

Common laws are laws that have been followed for many years, but have not been formally written down like constitutional laws.

Some legal terms explained

Degree of intent	If you are arrested and charged with a crime, how your crime will be judged will depend a lot on whether you intended to commit the crime or not.
An indictable offence	A serious offence, which usually leads to trial by jury.
A summary offence	A more minor offence, usually tried in the district court.
Larceny	Stealing.
Robbery	Using force or fear to steal, e.g. mugging.
Burglary	Stealing from a house or vehicle.
	(If any of these offences – larceny, robbery or burglary – is aggravated, this means that the criminal had a weapon.)
To be put on remand	This is when the judge does not pass sentence there and then, but will do so at a later date or else pass the case on to a higher court. People can either be remanded in custody (locked up) or remanded on conditional release with or without bail.
Bail	This is a sum of money paid to the courts by a friend or relation of a person accused of a crime. If the person does not turn up in court the next time, the bail money is lost.
The DPP (Director of Public Prosecutions)	This office looks at the book of evidence against an individual accused of a crime and decides whether there is enough evidence to go ahead and prosecute. If the office of the DPP thinks there is, they will prosecute on behalf of the people of Ireland.
In camera	All family law cases such as applications for barring orders, legal separations, etc. are held in camera, which means in private. The general public cannot attend.
Civil law case	An action taken by an individual against another individual or organisation usually for compensation, e.g. a man slips on a wet floor in a supermarket and breaks his leg. He may make a claim against the supermarket.
Criminal law case	Criminal law covers offences that are seen to be detrimental to society as a whole, e.g. assault. Such cases are prosecuted by the state through the DPP.

The Courts

The Irish court system

Supreme Court

Highest court
in the land.
Five judges.
Decisions made by this
court must be followed in the
future by lower courts.

High Court

Hears criminal and civil cases
(when hearing criminal cases it is called
the Central Criminal Court) and appeals
from lower courts. Sometimes a jury.
Decisions made by this court must be
followed in the future by lower courts.

Court of Criminal Appeal

Hears appeals from other courts.

Special Criminal Court

Three judges, no jury. Deals with terrorist-type offences.

Central Criminal Court

Really the High Court when it is hearing criminal cases.
Judge and jury. Hears serious criminal cases.

Circuit Court

Sometimes has a jury. Sometimes cases are sent here by the District Court judge.
This court also hears appeals against District Court decisions.

Children Court

Deals with cases involving under-18s. There is a separate children court in Smithfield, Dublin.
Outside Dublin, however, the children court is held at a special sitting of the District Court.
The media must not identify a young person appearing in this court.

District Court

Local court. More minor offences, no jury, usually a fine is imposed instead of a sentence. Deals with barring orders,
maintenance payments, etc. All family law cases are held 'in camera', which means in private. The maximum sentence for
an offence is 12 months, although this can go up to 24 months if you are being tried for more than one offence.

Understanding Your Rights and Responsibilities

- A member of the Gardaí can stop and search you in the street if they think you are in possession of an illegal drug.
- If you are arrested, you must give the Gardaí your correct name and address.
- If you are driving a car, motorbike or other vehicle, a guard can stop you, ask you to give your correct name and address, and to produce your licence and insurance within 10 days. You must also allow yourself to be breathalysed.
- If you are under 18 years of age, you must have a parent or other responsible adult there with you while being questioned by the Gardaí.
- If you are over 12 years of age, it is assumed that you know right from wrong.
- You have the right to talk to a solicitor.
- If there is a warrant for your arrest, the reason for your arrest will be written on it. You have the right to see this document.

Under the Education Welfare Act you must remain in full-time education until you have reached the age of 17, or 16 if you have a Junior Certificate or FETAC qualification. You should not without good reason (certified illness) miss any more than 20 days in any one school year.

ACTIVITY

Answer true or false to the following statements:	True	False
Stealing a bicycle is an indictable offence.	☐	☐
'In camera' means that TV cameras are permitted in the courtroom	☐	☐
If arrested, you can legally remain totally silent.	☐	☐
Larceny means deliberately burning down someone's building.	☐	☐
Aggravated assault means assault with a weapon.	☐	☐
Murder, rape and such crimes are tried in the District Court.	☐	☐
Decisions in the Supreme and High Court have implications for the lower courts.	☐	☐
There are occasions when you can be searched without a warrant.	☐	☐

Young people and the law

Garda statistics show that the types of offence committed most commonly by young people under the age of 18 are theft, alcohol-related offences, criminal damage, assault, traffic offences, drugs possession, public order offences and burglary. The Children Act 2001 is the main piece of legislation dealing with crime and under-18s.

The **Irish Youth Justice Service** was established in 2005 to help implement recommendations of the Children Act 2001 and to take overall responsibility for youth justice, co-ordinating all the other organisations involved, e.g. the Gardaí and the probation services. Their mission statement is:

> To create a safer society by working in partnership to reduce youth offending through appropriate interventions and linkages into services.

So how does the Irish Youth Justice Service work?

As mentioned above, the Children Act is the main piece of legislation dealing with youth justice. The main principles of the act in relation to young people and the law are:

- If a young person admits to and takes responsibility for what they have done they should not be charged (unless what they have done is very serious or they have offended repeatedly).
- Instead they may be cautioned and then referred to the Garda Juvenile Diversion Programme, where they will work with a specially trained garda called a Juvenile Liaison Officer (JLO), who will help them stay out of trouble. (In 2005 there were 17,567 young people referred to this programme, 75 per cent of whom managed to avoid a conviction.)
- The Gardaí are also involved in a variety of community-run Youth Diversion projects (mostly in the evenings, but in areas where there are very high numbers of early school leavers projects are run during the day). The idea behind these projects is to help young people at risk of offending to develop their sense of community and their social skills. It is hoped that this will help them choose not to offend.
- If a young person has to be charged, for example if they continue to offend or have committed a very serious offence, the courts will either have to refer the young person to the probation services or send them to a detention centre. Detention centres are used only as a very last resort (see below).
- Young people who are charged and referred to the probation services will be assigned a probation officer. Probation officers, like Garda JLOs, work with young people to help them keep out of trouble. The main difference is that JLOs work with young people who have only been cautioned, whereas probation officers work with young people who have been charged and convicted in court.
- If a young person has been convicted of a crime, then he or she may receive a **community sanction.** The probation services monitor the young person to make sure they are carrying out what was recommended by the community sanction. Community sanctions allow the young person to remain within their own community. There are a total of ten community sanctions available to the courts. Which one of these the judge chooses will depend on the nature of the offence and the young person's offending history. (See the list on the next page.)
- On 16 October 2006, under the Children Act 2001, the age of criminal responsibility was

effectively raised from seven to 12 years. Under the new provisions, no child under the age of 12 years can be charged with an offence. An exception is made for ten- and 11-year-olds charged with very serious offences, such as unlawful killing, a rape offence or aggravated sexual assault. In addition, the Director of Public Prosecutions (DPP) must give consent for any child under the age of 14 years to be charged.

Ten community sanctions

1. **Community service order:** young person (16–17 years old) agrees to complete unpaid work for a set total number of hours in the community.
2. **Day centre order:** young person must attend a centre (e.g. youth reach), taking part in a programme of activities.
3. **Probation order:** young person is closely supervised by a probation officer for a certain period of time. He/she must report to the probation officer at agreed times.
4. **Training or activities order:** young person must take part in a particular type of training or activity, e.g. anger management classes.
5. **Intensive supervision order:** young person is closely supervised by their probation officer and must take part in certain activities or perhaps attend a treatment programme, e.g. drugs or alcohol addiction services.
6. **Residential supervision order:** young person must live in a suitable hostel. The hostel must be close to where they live so they can continue their education.
7. **A suitable person order:** with agreement from the young person's parents or guardians the child is placed in the care of a suitable adult.
8. **A mentor (family) order:** the young people and his/her family are assigned help, advice and support to help stop the young person re-offending.
9. **A restriction of movement order:** this requires the young person to stay away from certain places (e.g. down town) and to be at a specific address between 7 p.m. and 6 a.m. daily.
10. **A dual order:** this combines a restriction of movement order with either supervision by a probation officer or attendance at a day centre.

Restorative justice programmes

In addition, young people who offend may be asked to meet with their victim and apologise for the hurt they have caused. The victim may be given the opportunity to speak to the young person to explain how the crime affected them. Sometimes the young person pays some form of compensation (for example, if a young person destroyed someone's car, they might pay the victim a sum of money every week towards the cost of getting it fixed), or they might do some work in the community.

The Children Court

There is a special court for children and young people who are in trouble with the law and who are being charged with a crime. The Children Court is where a judge listens to both sides about what happened and decides what to do.

Children Courts are held in the courtrooms where ordinary sittings of the District Court are held, except in Dublin, which has a dedicated Children Court. The sittings are held at different times from those for adults who have to come to the District Court.

The Children Court gives special attention to helping young people understand what is going on. If the parents or guardian cannot afford to pay a solicitor, the court can offer legal aid for the young person.

Children's detention schools – the last resort

Sometimes because of the type of offence(s) committed, the court will be forced to send a child to a place of detention. Before sending a child to detention, the court will try to make sure that there is no other option available that would address the offences which the young person has committed.

A young person can be ordered to be detained by the court to either a detention school or to St Patrick's Institution in Dublin. The courts will only sentence a young person to a detention school as a last resort.

The Children Act 2001 makes it illegal to order the detention in a prison of a young person under 18 years (with effect from 1 March 2007). There are currently four detention schools where a young person can be ordered to be detained by the courts. These are:

- Trinity House, Lusk
- Oberstown Boys' School, Lusk
- Oberstown Girls' School, Lusk
- Finglas Child and Adolescent Centre.

and
- St Patrick's Institution (for 16- and 17- year-old boys for a transitional period).

St Patrick's Institution

St Patrick's Institution is managed by the Irish Prison Service. At the moment, it is a closed institution for male offenders aged 16 to 21 years. Plans have been made for separate accommodation for the majority of 16- and 17-year-old boys, pending the further development of the children's detention schools.

 **ACTIVITY**

Read the three case studies below. Using the information you have gained from reading about youth justice in Ireland, say how you think each case should be dealt with by the Gardaí, courts and probation services.

Case study 1

Jill Salmon is 13 years old. She was suspended from school for the third time last week, this time for fighting – the teachers said she was bullying. On the Wednesday night she went up to the school and broke a load of windows. She would have got away with it but for one of the teachers who was working late and saw her.

_____

_____

_____

Case study 2

Andy Hickey is 15 years old. He has been in trouble with the law on and off since he was ten, mostly for drinking and possessing cannabis. Recently he was arrested with his friend Stephen for breaking the passenger windows of two cars parked at traffic lights and stealing the handbags off the seats. They got nearly €500 from the two bags, along with credit cards and mobile phones. They were spotted on CCTV footage and arrested. There is a family history of both unemployment and drink- and drugs-related offences.

_____

_____

_____

Case Study 3

Paul Jones is 16 years old. He has been in trouble with the law on and off since he was about 11, first for vandalism and more recently for drugs possession and for causing hassle when he is drunk. Paul has recently dropped out of school and spends most of the day in bed. He goes out most evenings but rarely comes home before two or three in the morning. Four weeks ago he was arrested for robbing a petrol station with a knife. Paul's parents are both professional people, but his father has a severe problem with alcohol. Paul's older brother has spent time in St Patrick's Institution, but now seems to be doing well.

_____

_____

_____

KEY ASSIGNMENT

For this key assignment you are required to take part with others in a roleplay about your civil rights. Below are some suggestions; you should try some of your own as well. It may be necessary to invite a local garda or JLO to talk to your group and advise you about civil rights before doing your roleplay.

You are walking along the street drinking out of a can of cider. You have a bag with three or more cans in it. A garda stops you.

A squad car pulls up at your house. The gardaí believe that you have some stolen CDs in your possession.

You have been arrested for shoplifting and you are now in the police station. You have the stolen goods on you.

You are refused entry to a shop in town.

You are a passenger in a stolen car. The gardaí catch up with you and arrest you, the two other passengers and the driver.

When you have completed this key assignment, go to page 197 and tick off Assignment 6 on the checklist.

EXAM TIME

Social Education (2005) – short question
1. Remanded in custody means?
Out on bail   Locked up   Conditional release

Social Education (2006) – short question
2. Below is a list of four of the main courts in Ireland

District court   High court   Circuit court   Supreme court

Select any **two** courts from the list above and describe the work of each.

Court: _____

Work: _____

Court: _____

Work: _____

Social Education (2008) – short question
3. A Civil Law case is:

Taken by an individual against another individual or organisation

Prosecuted by the state through the DPP

A trial by a community group against one of its members

UNIT 6 Contemporary Issue Task

This task should be completed during session 3, in Year 2. For this task you are asked to investigate a contemporary issue of importance to you. Tasks may be undertaken as a group, but if they are your own individual contribution (what you actually did on your own) this must be made very clear to the examiner. Unlike some others, this task has three parts. If one or more parts are left out, marks will be lost. The three parts are:

1. Written task report: where you write about how you investigated your contemporary issue and what you found out.

2. Action: here you must carry out an action designed to (1) inform people about your issue and/or (2) do something to help or improve your issue.

3. Oral presentation: at the beginning of your interview you must make a short speech (2–4 minutes) about the issue you have chosen.

The Task Report

Your task report will have to contain sections on each of the following. This list may be useful as a table of contents.

1. Statement of aims

2. Planning

3. Research

4. Carrying out the action

5. Summary and analysis of findings

6. Evaluation and self-evaluation

7. Appendix.

Stage 1 Deciding what to do

This goes into your planning section.

ACTIVITY

As a group, brainstorm for interesting contemporary issues. Record what you come up with below.

From this list pick the issue that you feel interests you most. Note: You may have to research a few issues before you can make this decision.

I chose _____ as my contemporary issue because

_____

Stage 2 Write out your list of aims

What do you hope to achieve by doing this task?

If yours is a group task, you must record group and individual aims.

Sample list of aims – issue: Problems facing Travellers today

Aims

- I aim to find out more about the issues and problems facing Travellers in Ireland today, e.g. health, housing, education and discrimination.
- I aim to interview a Traveller from my area about their life and what being a Traveller means to them.
- I aim to find out more about Travellers in other countries, e.g. Roma, and make comparisons with Irish Travellers.
- I aim to find out more about Traveller interest groups.

- I aim to make a presentation to my classmates so that they will be better informed about problems facing Travellers.
- I aim to carry out this task in an organised way so that I am happy with the work I have done and am finished on time.

Stage 3 Planning: what are you going to do and when are you going to do it?

This task should take a total of ten hours to complete. This is not very long, so it is important that you decide early on what it is you have to do and make a plan for carrying work out.

Essential jobs

1. Research: Two types of research have to be undertaken for this task.

    - Primary research, e.g. interviews, surveys, questionnaires.

    - Secondary research – getting information from the Internet, from newspapers or books.

2. You must look at your issue from at least two of the following perspectives:

    - local
    - national
    - global.

    In the Traveller example, the issue is examined from all three perspectives.

3. You must read all the research material that you gather and summarise and analyse your findings. There is no sense in having chunks of material from the Internet or from books if you have not read it and shown you understand it.

4. You must think of and carry out an action relating to your issue.

5. You must prepare a short speech (2-4 minutes) about your chosen issue for the examiner.

6. You must first evaluate how well you achieved your aims (task evaluation) and carry out a self-evaluation.

Module SIX

Taking Charge

This module should be completed during session 4 (Year 2).

Below are the four key assignments for Module 6. You must do ALL of these. As you work through this module and complete each one, come back to this page and tick it off.

1. I prepared a step-by-step guide to leaving home and finding a place to live. I included the different considerations that need to be taken into account.

    Date: ___ /___ /_____

2. I conducted and recorded (either on tape or in writing) an interview with a young person living away from home.

    Date: ___ /___ /_____

3. I prepared a weekly budget for a young person living on his or her own. I based this budget on the current weekly wage of a young person who has just started working.

    Date: ___ /___ /_____

4. As part of a group, I participated in a discussion with a visitor representing a bank, credit union or building society, and reported on what I learned from the discussion.

    Date: ___ /___ /_____

A Place of My Own

Moving out of home for the first time can be both an exciting and a daunting time. In this unit we will be looking at the options, challenges and problems that a young person may face when they decide to take that first big step.

KEY ASSIGNMENT

Prepare a step-by-step guide to leaving home and finding a place to live. Include the different considerations that need to be taken into account. Complete the activities and listening exercises in this unit to fulfil the requirements of this key assignment.

When you have completed this key assignment, go to page 251 and tick off Assignment 1 on the checklist.

Reasons for Moving Out

It is important that when young people decide to move out of home it is for a good reason and not because they feel that they have to, even though they do not want to or are not really ready to. This can lead to a disaster and much hardship and unhappiness for everyone involved.

ACTIVITY

Look at the list below of some of the more common reasons given for moving out of home. Tick whether you think the reason given is a good one or a bad one. Good reasons usually mean that the person has thought about what he or she is doing. Bad reasons tend to be the result of snap or emotional decisions.

	Good reason	Bad reason
To get away from nagging parents	☐	☐
To be able to come and go as I please	☐	☐
To be independent	☐	☐
To have a wild time drinking and going out	☐	☐
So my boy/girlfriend can sleep with me	☐	☐
To be near work/college	☐	☐
To get away from a violent or abusive home	☐	☐
To prove that I don't need anybody	☐	☐

Where to Live

When a young person decides to move out of home and find a place to live, money is usually the biggest factor that needs consideration when deciding on the type of accommodation that is most suitable. Even though you may pay some money to your parent(s) for your keep, it is usually only when you move out that the real cost of living becomes apparent to most people.

⚙ ACTIVITY

Here is a list of the usual types of accommodation available for renting. Look at each of them and then decide which of them would be (a) the most expensive and (b) the most suitable for a person moving out of home for the first time on a limited budget.

- Purpose-built flat or apartment
- Digs
- Self-contained flat within a large house
- Flat within a large house with some shared facilities
- Bedroom in a house with all other facilities shared
- Bedsit.

1. Which of these options would be the most expensive? _____
2. Which of these options would be the most suitable for a young person moving out of home for the first time? _____

Give a reason for your answer: _____

Cost, while usually the biggest factor in deciding on where to live, is not the only factor. Put a tick beside the factors below that would be important to you.

Having my own bedroom ☐
Not having to share a bathroom ☐
Not having to share kitchen/sitting room ☐
Good state of repair ☐
Washing machine ☐
Central heating ☐
Telephone ☐
Digital TV ☐
Near shops, pubs, etc. ☐
Near work/college ☐
Tastefully decorated ☐
Garden ☐

 **ACTIVITY**

Threshold is an organisation that provides information for tenants and landlords. They have a very informative website (www.threshold.ie) and also have a number of regional centres. Someone from the class could be nominated to phone Threshold to ask them for copies of some of their information leaflets.

Dublin	21 Stoneybatter, Dublin 7	(01) 678 6096
Cork	22 South Mall	(021) 427 8848
Galway	3 Victoria Place, Merchant's Road	(091) 563080
Limerick	26 Catherine Street	(061) 405400

Finding a Place to Rent

If you are looking for a place to rent, you could try each of the following options:

- The 'to let' sections of local or evening papers, e.g. the *Evening Herald*.
- Ads in shop windows around the area you want to rent in.
- 'To let' signs on the actual buildings.
- If you are a student, 'to let' signs on the college notice board.
- Word of mouth.
- Estate and letting agents.

 **ACTIVITY**

Look at the classified advertisement and answer the questions that follow.

> **ADJ O'Connell St, D1,** Gresham Hse, 1 bed, 2nd flr, own pkg space, F/F GFCH, p.tv, wash/dryer, profs only. €900pm, min 1 year.
> Ph: (086) 767 9543

What do you think these abbreviations in the ad mean?

Own pkg space _____	F/F _____
p.tv _____	min 1 year _____
GFCH _____	profs only _____

ACTIVITY

Look up three places to let in your local area. A small group from your class might want to visit an estate agent or look through a copy of your local paper and telephone to find out the following information about the accommodation.

	Address	Rent	Deposit due	Facilities
1.				
2.				
3.				

Viewing accommodation

CD - Track 23

Fiona and Catherine are viewing a flat. Listen to the conversation they have with the landlord and then the one they have between themselves in private. Tick the items from the list below that they remember to check out.

General area
Bus routes
Local shops, laundrette, etc.
Pubs and other recreational facilities
Is the area relatively safe?

The flat itself
How much is the rent?
How much deposit has to be paid?
What are the arrangements for rent collection?
Are there any signs of dampness?
How would you get out in the event of a fire?

Do the windows open?

Is there good ventilation?

Details of arrangements for heating the flat

Are the beds and other items of furniture in
good condition?

Is there enough storage space?

Are all the appliances working?

What are the facilities for washing clothes?

Is there a list of all the items in the flat (an inventory)?

How is the water heated?

How are bills paid?

Who cleans the common areas?

Who else has keys to the flat?

Is the flat hooked up for TV?

Outside

Is there access to the garden and clothes line?

Who takes care of rubbish disposal?

Where can bikes and prams be stored?

Who does the garden?

Rent books and leases

A lease is an oral or written agreement made between the tenant and the landlord. Because rent books are now required by law, there may be no separate lease. The lease is usually part of and written into the rent book. The primary function of a rent book is to record payments made by the tenant to the landlord, although the following additional information must by law be included:

- Name and address of the rented dwelling.
- Name and address of the landlord or his agent.
- Name of the tenant(s).
- Length of the tenancy (often one year).
- The amount of rent and how it is to be paid (cash, cheque, standing order, etc.).
- Who is responsible for payments other than rent, e.g. electricity bills, telephone.
- The amount of the deposit and under what circumstances it will be returned.
- An inventory of contents.
- The date the tenancy starts (the date you move in).

In addition to the above it is usually wise to clarify with the landlord each of the following points:

- Under what circumstances the landlord can enter the premises. Ask that he or she does not enter without contacting you first and without you being present.
- An emergency phone number.
- What repairs the landlord is responsible for.

ACTIVITY

In a previous activity you looked in your local papers and in estate agencies for three places to let. Imagine you decided to move into one of them. You are now signing the lease. Fill in the sample lease form below. You will have to make up some of the information.

Address of Premises	**Tenancy Details**			
	Date of commencement	Day	Month	Year
	Deposit paid	€		
	Rent paid in advance	€		
Name and address of Landlord	Term of tenancy (tick one)	Rent	Rent day	
	☐ Weekly	€		
	☐ Monthly	(per week/month)		
	☐ Fixed term	From Day	Month	Year
Landlord's telephone no. (optional)		To Day	Month	Year
Name and address of landlord's agent (if applicable)	Payment by: (tick one)			
	Cash ☐		Cheque ☐	
	Standing order ☐			
	Landlord's bank and account number (if relevant)			
Agent's telephone no. (optional)				
	Account No ☐☐☐☐☐☐☐☐☐			
Name(s) of tenant(s)	Deposits are returned at the end of tenancy. Landlords may make reasonable deductions for damage done above normal wear and tear, outstanding bills and/or inadequate notice.			
	Payments for services not included in rent			

Service	Frequency of payment

(services include electricity, gas, TV, phone, etc.

Signed _____

Signed _____

              Landlord/Agent

              Tenants

Tenant and landlord rights and responsibilities

 CD - Track 24

Jane has heard so many bad stories about landlords mistreating tenants that she has decided to ring Threshold and get the facts straight. Listen to the conversation on Track 24 and then answer the questions below.

1. Can the landlord increase my rent? _____

2. Does the landlord have to supply me with a rent book? _____

3. Does the landlord have to give notice if he/she wants me out? _____

4. How much notice must I give the landlord if I wish to leave and have not agreed to any fixed period in a lease? _____

5. If I signed a lease for a year and want to leave before the year is up, what risks am I taking?
_____

6. What should I do if my accommodation is in very bad condition?_____

7. Can the landlord enter the premises whenever he or she chooses?_____

8. Under what circumstances can the landlord refuse to return my deposit?
_____

9. What are the rules about other people staying in the accommodation?
_____

Running a Home

 ACTIVITY

Joanne and Mary are sharing a two-bedroom house in Dublin. Both of them are student nurses in a nearby hospital. Make a list of duties or tasks in the home for them and use this list to come up with a monthly roster. Make out the roster, ensuring that each one does their fair share of work and that one person is not doing the same job all the time. Some jobs will have to be done every day; others need doing less often.

Sharing with others – potential problems

 **ACTIVITY**

Read each of the four problem situations below. Write down the course of action you would take to help solve each of them. Think of other examples and discuss them in small groups.

Situation 1

The landlord collects the rent on a Friday evening at seven o'clock. One of your flatmates, who is also a good friend, goes to the pub with her workmates on a Friday evening and is never there to pay her share of the rent. You usually end up paying it for her and while she pays you back eventually, you are sometimes stuck for cash between times. It is annoying you.
What should you do? _____
_____

Situation 2

You live in a house with two other people. For the most part you get along really well. Lately, though, you have been getting really annoyed when you go to take a bath. There is always scum around the edge after one of the other two has used it. You always clean the bath until it's spotless so you don't see why you should have to clean it before you get into it as well.
What should you do? _____
_____

Situation 3

You share a flat with a good friend of yours. Things were going really well until she got herself a new boyfriend. He is never out of the place. You walk into the sitting room to watch TV and there they are cuddling on the couch. They look at you as if you are intruding and make you feel uncomfortable. You now spend most of the evening stuck in your room.
What should you do? _____
_____

Situation 4

Your flatmate is always using your toiletries and washing powder without asking. Neither of you has much money. You feel unfairly treated.

What should you do? _____

_____

 **KEY ASSIGNMENT**

For this key assignment you are required to record (either on tape or in writing) an interview with a young person living away from home. Make a list of things you feel would be important to ask. You could include some of the questions listed below along with some of your own.

When you have completed this key assignment, go to page 251 and tick off Assignment 2 on the checklist.

1. Would you describe the accommodation that you have at present as good/fair/poor?
2. How much rent do you pay per week?
3. How much on average do you have to spend on essentials every week?
4. What do you see as the main advantage of living away from home?
5. What do you see as the main disadvantage of living away from home?
6. What is your daily routine?
7. What do you do in your free time?
8. Do you find yourself going out to pubs and clubs more or less often now you are not at home?
9. What advice would you give someone thinking of moving out of home?

 **EXAM TIME**

Social Education (2005) – short question

1. A leaseholder's rent can be increased:
   As much and as often as the landlord wishes
   Only at the start of the lease agreement
   Every twelve months only

Social Education (2005) – long question (part)

2. Mark Moloney is a 19-year-old trainee tool maker. He is thinking of moving out of home and is earning €300 per week.

    (a) What type of accommodation should Mark look for? Give a reason for your choice.

        Type of accommodation: _____

        Reason: _____

    (b) List **two** rights that Mark will have in the accommodation he chooses.

        1. _____

        2. _____

    (c) Name an agency which provides support/advice if difficulties arise regarding accommodation.

        _____

Social Education (2006) – long question (part)

3. 'The Housing Act 1992 states that a landlord must provide a rent book. This will record rent paid. Other things recorded include an inventory of contents, the length of tenancy, the deposit.'

    (a) Select **two** of the 'other things' mentioned above and explain each.

        Item: _____

        Explain: _____

        Item: _____

        Explain: _____

    (b) List **two** pieces of information, not mentioned in 3(a), that should be contained in a rent book.

        1. _____

        2. _____

Social Education (2007) – short question

4. A landlord must give a minimum 'notice to quit' of:

        Two weeks   Four weeks   Six weeks

Social Education (2007) – long question

5. (a) Select **one** type of rented accommodation for a young person who is moving out of home. Give **two** reasons why you think this is a better choice than the others. (Tick (✓) your choice).

    Lodgings/digs   Hostel   Semi-detached house   Flat

        1. _____

        2. _____

(b) Case study:

John has been renting a flat for eight months. When he started renting this flat he signed a lease agreement for twelve months. Now his landlord wants him out in two weeks. John was told this when his landlord phoned him. He informed John that he would not be getting his deposit back as the place would need to be cleaned and painted once John leaves. When John told him that he could not possibly get somewhere else to stay and be moved in two weeks the landlord informed him that he would remove John's belongings from the flat and change the locks if he did not co-operate.

Why is John legally entitled to stay in the flat for twelve months?

_____

It is not reasonable for the landlord to keep John's deposit because of normal 'wear and tear'. When is it reasonable for a landlord to keep a tenant's deposit?

_____

The landlord said 'he would remove John's belongings from the flat and change the locks if he did not co-operate'. What are John's legal entitlements in this situation?

_____

_____

Social Education (2008) – long question (part)

6. (a) Other than contact details, mention one other piece of information which a rent book must include.

_____

(b) Why is it important for tenants to read the contents of a lease before signing it?

_____

_____

_____

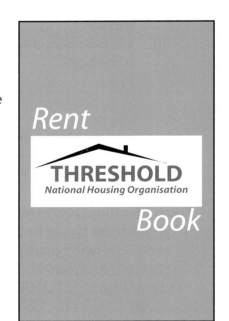

Rent

THRESHOLD
National Housing Organisation

Book

UNIT 2 Making Ends Meet

A Balanced Diet on a Budget

 **ACTIVITY**

Make up a five-day menu for a young person living away from home. Include breakfast, lunch, an evening meal and a selection of healthy snacks. Make out a shopping list for this five-day menu. Go to the local supermarket and price all the items on the list. What total did you get?

Keep your five-day menu and your shopping list in your Social Education folder as it will be useful for completing the next key assignment in this unit.

Organising Your Finances

When you are living away from home it is very important for your health and happiness that essential bills such as rent, electricity, food and gas are paid before you spend money on less important items such as non-essential clothing and entertainment. Often it is wise to set up direct debit and standing order mandates for these essential bills. Basically what happens is that money for these bills is taken out of your bank account at a specified time each month (or every two months with some household bills, e.g. electricity). Once all essential bills are paid you then have an accurate idea of how much money you have to spend on other things.

KEY ASSIGNMENT

Prepare a weekly budget for a young person living on his or her own. Base this budget on the current weekly wage of a young person who has just started working.

When you have completed this key assignment, go to page 251 and tick off Assignment 3 on the checklist.

Go down to your local job centre, or look in the local papers. Find three jobs advertised that would suit a young person who has just completed their Leaving Certificate Applied.

Description of Job	Pay
Job 1	
Job 2	
Job 3	

Imagine you were to take one of the jobs above. Try to work out a weekly budget based on the wage offered by this job. Below is a list of common expenses incurred by people living away from home. Estimate the average weekly cost of each one. Then see if your budget balances. If it doesn't, you will have to think of ways of making savings.

Clothes　　　　　　　　　　＿＿＿＿＿
Transport　　　　　　　　　　＿＿＿＿＿
Nights out　　　　　　　　　　＿＿＿＿＿
Hobbies　　　　　　　　　　＿＿＿＿＿
Toiletries　　　　　　　　　　＿＿＿＿＿
Cigarettes　　　　　　　　　　＿＿＿＿＿
Breakfasts　　　　　　　　　　＿＿＿＿＿
Work lunches　　　　　　　　＿＿＿＿＿
Evening meals　　　　　　　　＿＿＿＿＿
Rent　　　　　　　　　　　　＿＿＿＿＿
Electricity　　　　　　　　　　＿＿＿＿＿
Heating　　　　　　　　　　＿＿＿＿＿
Telephone　　　　　　　　　　＿＿＿＿＿
TV rental　　　　　　　　　　＿＿＿＿＿
Laundry　　　　　　　　　　＿＿＿＿＿
(this could be going to the laundrette or buying washing powder)

Total income　　　＝　　　＿＿＿＿＿

Total expenditure　＝　　　＿＿＿＿＿

Balance　　　　　＝　　　＿＿＿＿＿

Did your income cover your expenditure　　　　　Yes　　　　　　No
If it didn't, where could you make savings?

_____

_____

🔧 ACTIVITY

You are now in the final year of your Leaving Certificate Applied. Imagine yourself in two to three years' time when you have completed any other courses and have moved out of home. Think about a realistic career that you would like. Find out how much this career pays to someone starting out. Plan a comprehensive and realistic annual budget for yourself.

🔧 ACTIVITY

Make a list of leisure activities that you could participate in which cost little or no money.

_____
_____
_____

UNIT 3 Account Options

Using Cash Only

🔧 ACTIVITY

In the past it was mainly the well-off who had bank accounts, cheque books, etc. The majority of ordinary people operated on a cash-only basis. Their wages were paid in cash and they bought and paid for everything in cash. One good effect of this was that not very many people got into severe debt. You could only spend what you had in your pocket. Having said that, operating on a cash-only basis has its disadvantages. Can you name some of them in the space below?

_____
_____
_____
_____

KEY ASSIGNMENT

Most banks and building societies have an education officer. For this key assignment you must invite the education officer or another official of a bank, building society or credit union to visit your school or centre. Prepare for the visit by making a list of questions you would like to ask him or her. Afterwards, report back on what you learned from the visit. Record some of the things you learned below.

When you have completed this key assignment, go to page 251 and tick off Assignment 4 on the checklist.

Five things I learned from the visit are:

1. _____
2. _____
3. _____
4. _____
5. _____

The Credit Union

History

The first credit unions in Ireland were opened in 1958. In the beginning there were only three credit unions in Ireland; today there are over 520 with over 1.8 million members. A credit union is not a building but a group of people who have decided to save together and lend money to each other at reasonable rates of interest. These transactions just take place in the building that you call the credit union. Credit unions are unlike banks or building societies in that members have what is called a common bond. This common

bond means that the members of a particular credit union have something between them that unites them. This could be that they all live in the one area, they all have the same occupation (e.g. the teachers' credit union), or perhaps that all the members belong to a particular society or association.

When you join a credit union, you become one of its owners, and have a say in how it is run. Once you join and pay the usual fee of €1 you are a shareholder and are entitled to vote at the annual general meeting. At the end of the year the profits (called dividends) made by the credit union are divided up among its members. The more shares you have (that is, the more you have saved), the bigger the dividend you will receive. When you have been saving with your credit union for a period of time, you can take out a loan.

⚙ ACTIVITY

Visit your local credit union and find out the following information.

1. When was this credit union founded? _____

2. How long do you have to be saving before you can take out a loan?
   _____

3. What is the present rate of interest on loans? _____

4. How long does it take for a decision to be made on your loan?
   _____

5. What age do you have to be to join the credit union in your own name?
   _____

6. What are the opening hours of this credit union?
   _____

7. Apart from savings and lending what other services does this credit union offer?
   _____
   _____

8. If you have saved €300 how much could you expect to be allowed to borrow?
   _____

9. What is the procedure for getting a loan from your credit union?
   _____
   _____
   _____

10. What other advantages are there to being a credit union member as opposed to being a member of a bank? _____
    _____
    _____
    _____

When you visit your credit union, complete the following forms:

- application for membership
- loan application form
- lodgement form
- withdrawal form.

Although this module requires you to fill in the forms for membership but not necessarily become a member, it might be a good idea to take this opportunity to join your local credit union.

Banking

Nowadays it is becoming more and more necessary to have a bank account. As a result, banks now offer a greater number and variety of services. In this section we will look at each of the following:

Deposit accounts ☐
Current accounts ☐
Cheque books and cheque cards ☐
Direct debit as a payment method ☐
Standing orders as a payment method ☐
Credit cards ☐
Laser cards ☐
Automated teller machines (ATMs) ☐
24-hour banking ☐

When you have worked through this unit and think you know what each of the above is, tick the box beside it to indicate this.

Deposit accounts

These accounts are also called savings accounts. Although some people use these accounts for all their business they were originally designed for savings: the account holder would lodge money into the account and leave it there to gather interest. Usually the same forms are used to open deposit accounts and current accounts. An example is given below. All you have to do is tick 'deposit' or 'current' to indicate which type of account you wish to open.

Note: To open an account you will need photographic ID, for example a passport, and proof of your address.

ACTIVITY

Fill out the application form below. It is similar to the form you would be asked to fill out if you wanted to open either a deposit (savings) or current account.

Account required	Savings/deposit ☐	Current ☐

Personal details

Surname	
First name(s)	
Address for correspondence	
Telephone	(H) (W)
Date of birth	
Marital status	single ☐ married ☐ other ☐
No. of dependent children	
Do you (tick one)	
Own your home ☐	
Rent your home ☐	
Live with parents ☐	
Other ☐	
If you are a student when will you qualify?	
What course are you studying?	

Employment details

Occupation

Take home pay €

Employer's name and address

Details of other accounts

If you have another account in this bank what is your account number?
☐ ☐ ☐ ☐ ☐ ☐ ☐ ☐

If you have an account at another bank state the bank and which branch.

Do you have any of the following?

Visa ☐   Mastercard ☐   Other credit card ☐

Have you a mortgage?   Yes ☐   No ☐

If yes, how much is it for? €

Signature

Date

Current accounts

Current accounts are designed to be working accounts. There is no interest paid on current accounts so money does not usually stay in them for long. Most people have a deposit account and a current account. They put spare money into their deposit account and leave it there until they need the money for something special. The current account is for everyday use.

Paying money into your current account

Usually the same form, called a lodgement slip, is used to lodge money into either a current account or a deposit or savings account. All you do is tick the 'current account' box instead of the 'savings account' box.

ACTIVITY

Visit your local bank and ask them for two lodgement slips.

Fill in each of the slips as follows:

Slip 1

Lodge a €144 cheque to your current account. You must make up the account number, the name of the bank and its branch.

Slip 2

Lodge €65 cash to your deposit or savings account. Again, make up any numbers, etc. that you may need.

Pay path

In addition to lodging money yourself into your current account, your employer can lodge your wages directly into your current account by what is called 'pay path'. To use this facility your employer will ask you to fill out a form giving your bank details, and this form will be sent to your employer's bank, telling them where to lodge your wages every week or month. Sometimes bank loans are easier to get if your wages come in by pay path. Can you think why this should be?

Taking money out of your current account

As a current account is for everyday use there are many ways in which money can be quickly and easily withdrawn or transferred from it. Here are some of the most common methods:

- cheque book and cheque card
- direct debit mandates
- standing orders
- bank giros
- laser cards
- 24-hour banking.

Cheque book and cheque guarantee card

While cheque books and cheque guarantee cards are not as commonly used as they once were, if you have a current account you may wish to apply for a cheque book and cheque guarantee card to pay for goods in establishments that do not have laser or credit card facilities. Usually cheques can only be used to pay for goods and services if you can provide a cheque guarantee card (usually the card will guarantee a cheque up to €130). A cheque guarantee card guarantees the retailer that the cheque won't bounce. There is a fee imposed for using cheques – so they are not normally used for small amounts.

ACTIVITY

You want to purchase a stereo in a local music shop called The Sound Shop. It costs €79.99. Write out a cheque for that amount. You would have to produce a cheque guarantee card. The retailer or shopkeeper copies down the number of the cheque guarantee card on the back of the cheque. This will ensure that the cheque will not bounce.

Direct debit

A direct debit mandate is an instruction you give your bank to pay out an unfixed amount of money from your account on a regular basis. Electricity bills, phone bills, mortgage payments, etc. can all be paid by direct debit. This means that you will never forget about them and they will be paid on time.

Standing order

A standing order is much like a direct debit mandate except with a standing order the amount paid out is always the same. A standing order could be set up to pay your rent every month. If you were paying fixed amounts for a car loan over a period of time, you could set up a standing order.

ACTIVITY

Visit your local bank and ask for a direct debit form and a standing order mandate. Fill in each of them for the following:

1. You are forever forgetting to pay your phone bill so you decide to set up a direct debit from your current account (you will have to make up the account numbers, bank and branch).

Can you think of two other bills that could be paid using direct debit?

1. _____   2. _____

2. You have taken out an insurance policy on your new car. It was very expensive, so you decided not to pay it all at once but to spread payments over the year. You are required to pay €126 per month. Fill in a standing order mandate instructing your bank to make this payment to your insurance company, which is Smart Drivers Insurance Ltd.

Can you think of two other bills that could be paid using a standing order?

1. _____   2. _____

Credit cards

Credit cards allow the cardholder to purchase goods and services up to a certain credit limit using the card. Credit limits usually start at around €750 and then increase, if you show the bank that you can use the card wisely and pay your bills on time. Credit card companies usually give you the option of paying off your bill in full each month or just paying a percentage of what you owe. It is best if you pay your bill off in full

every month, so that interest will not be charged on goods or services purchased on the card during that month. The exception to this is if you have withdrawn cash on your card. In this case, interest is charged from the day you withdraw the money.

How a credit card works

When your credit card is swiped through the electronic card reader in, for example, a supermarket, the machine reads the information that is held on the magnetic strip on the back of the card. This strip holds information such as how much your credit limit is and how much of this limit has been used up. It will also contain information on whether the card has been reported stolen. If you have gone over your limit or someone is trying to use a stolen card, the electronic card reader will not authorise the sale and you will not be able to purchase the goods.

Some shops have a manual machine as opposed to an electronic one. The shopkeeper must telephone the credit card company to check whether the card is OK.

Credit cards can be used in almost every country in the world. They are a valuable asset when travelling abroad. If you ran out of money while on holiday, someone at home could lodge money into your credit card account and you would be able to use your card almost immediately even if you were thousands of miles away. Credit cards can also be used for paying for goods on the Internet.

At the end of each month credit card holders get a credit card statement. This statement lists all the purchases made during the month, totals them and states the date to pay by.

Laser cards

Many people who have a current account also have what is called a laser card. This card is swiped through a machine at a cash desk, you enter a PIN number and the money is taken out of your current account soon after. Laser cards can be used in many different places such as shops, restaurants and petrol stations. Unlike a credit card, when you use a laser card you are not borrowing on credit but just accessing money already in your bank account.

ATMs

ATM stands for automated teller machine. Common ATMs are Banklink, Pass and Servicetill. Most people use ATMs for one purpose only, which is withdrawing cash. These machines, however, have the capacity to do much more than this – for example, you can:

- transfer money between accounts
- lodge money
- pay bills
- get your account balance
- request a full statement to be sent to you
- get a mini statement
- request a new chequebook.

To use these facilities you need an ATM card and a PIN number. (PIN stands for personal identification number.)

Some people have multi-purpose bank cards. One card can be an ATM card, a laser card and a cheque guarantee card all at the same time.

24-hour banking

ATM machines can be used 24 hours a day, 365 days a year. In addition to this, 24-hour telephone and Internet banking now means that a whole range of banking services are available to the public without leaving the comfort of their armchair. If you want to use telephone or Internet banking, you will need a security number which you will be asked for before you will be allowed to use any banking services. This is to guarantee the security of your account.

The Post Office

The following financial services are offered at present by the Post Office:

- prize bonds
- instalment savings scheme
- various deposit or savings accounts
- savings certificates
- savings bonds
- credit card service
- money transfer and order service
- bill payment
- bureau de change
- saving schemes for children (Cyril Squirrel)
- insurance.

ACTIVITY

Visit your local post office or go online at www.anpost.ie and find out the following information about the financial services they offer.

1. What are prize bonds?

2. What is the main advantage of prize bonds?

3. Would you consider that investing your money in prize bonds is a good way of saving? Give a reason for your answer.

4. How much money do you need to start buying prize bonds?

5. With the An Post 'instalment savings scheme', how often do you put money into the Post Office?
   Every day
   Every week
   Every month

6. What is the minimum amount that you can invest in each instalment?

7. Would you consider investing your money in this scheme? Give a reason for your answer.

8. What rate of interest does this scheme guarantee if you keep saving for five years or more? _____

9. Get an application form for a post office deposit account and fill it out. When you have done this tick the box opposite.

10. List two advantages of using the An Post 'pay a bill service'.

   _____

   _____

11. List six different bills that can be paid using this service.

   (a) _____   (d) _____

   (b) _____   (e) _____

   (c) _____   (f) _____

12. What age do you have to be to get an An Post credit card?

   _____

13. What is the Western Union Money Transfer service?
   Describe what you find out below.

   _____

   _____

   _____

14. What is a bureau de change?

   _____

15. Were you surprised at the variety of different services offered by the Post Office?

   Yes   No

Building societies

In the past building societies largely concerned themselves with mortgages and investment schemes. As a result of market demands, though, many have expanded their services to include some or all of the following:

- smaller personal loans
- insurance – home, life and travel
- bureau de change
- pensions
- savings accounts
- some have ATM facilities.

Name a building society in your town/area: _____

 **ACTIVITY**

Imagine you have €500 to invest. Investigate which institution provides the best investment option.

Institution that provides the best option: _____

EXAM TIME

Social Education (2005) – long question (part)

1. Mark Moloney is a 19-year-old trainee tool maker. He is thinking of moving out of home and is earning €300 per week. He wishes to save to go on holidays with friends to Spain and to get a credit card.

    (a) Mark could open his savings account with the Credit Union, the Post Office or the Bank. Which should he choose? Explain why.

    Name of Institution _____

    Explain: _____

    _____

    (b) Now that Mark has a steady income he wants to get a credit card. List **two** advantages and **two** disadvantages of a credit card for Mark.

    Advantages

    (1) _____

    (2) _____

    Disadvantages

    (1) _____

    (2) _____

Social Education (2006) – short questions

2. A PIN number is used to:

    Log on to an email account

    Access a bank account

    Register for social welfare payments

3. When cash is withdrawn from a credit card account which of the following is true?

    Interest is charged from the day that you withdraw the money

    Interest is not charged if your bill is paid off in full at the end of the month

    Interest is charged from the date your statement is issued

4. List **two** ways in which the Credit Union differs from banks.

    1. _____

    2. _____

5. **Social Education (2008) – long question (part)**

Credit cards – Gateway to Luxury or Gateway to Debt? A few months ago Sue's friend told her that she should get a credit card and that this would allow her to improve her wardrobe and her social life. Her mother thought that this was really a bad idea as Sue was barely paying her bills as it was. She warned her that credit cards were expensive and just paying the minimum payment could lead her into serious debt.

Now it seems that her mother was right. It was all so easy in the beginning and Sue loved being able to go out when she wanted. While she probably did not need all those new clothes, it was nice to be able to walk into a shop and buy whatever she wanted. Sue had a great summer but now finds that her credit card has reached its limit. Even though she is making the minimum payment each month her bill does not seem to be getting any smaller. Making ends meet for the winter is beginning to look increasingly difficult.

(a) How might Sue have managed her credit card better?

_____

_____

(b) 'Even though she is making the minimum payment each month her bill does not seem to be getting any smaller.' Why is this the case?

_____

_____

(c) List **two** pieces of advice you would give Sue to help her solve her current problem. State the reason why you would advise her to take this action.

Advice 1: _____

Reason: _____

Advice 2: _____

Reason: _____

UNIT 4 Saving and Borrowing

Borrowing

People frequently want to buy items that they do not have the money for. They have two options – saving for the item or borrowing for it. There are advantages and disadvantages to each. If you have to save for an item, you will have to wait until you have saved enough to pay for the item – this is the main disadvantage. The main advantage of borrowing is that you can have the item quickly. There are, however, two main disadvantages to borrowing. First, because of interest charged the item will cost considerably more in the end; and second, there is a risk that the borrower could get into debt, and perhaps be unable to meet loan repayments.

Sometimes borrowers will apply for loans and not really think through how they will repay them. This is why lenders (banks, etc.) generally allow a 'cooling-off period', usually ten days, during which the borrower can turn down the loan.

Sometimes lending institutions, e.g. banks, will ask a young person to provide a guarantor before they will agree to give them a loan. A guarantor (usually a parent) agrees to repay the loan if the borrower fails to repay it.

ACTIVITY

For this activity, you need to select an expensive item and look at options for acquiring it.

Selected item_____

Price of item_____

Saving

In the previous unit you took a general look at the various financial institutions. For this activity pick three of them, perhaps a bank, the Post Office and a credit union. Find out what rates of interest they offer on savings accounts.

Financial institution	Rate of interest on savings account
_____	_____
_____	_____
_____	_____

When you have found out which financial institution offers the best interest rate, decide how much you can afford to save every week. To do this calculate your average weekly income and your average weekly expenditure and take one from the other.

Weekly saving scheme for purchase of _____

Income	Expenditure
_____	_____
_____	_____
_____	_____
_____	_____
Total_____	Total_____

Total weekly income_____

Total weekly expenditure_____

Balance _____

Number of weeks to save for item_____

Borrowing

Investigate the possibility of getting a loan for the item. If you are under 18 years of age this might prove difficult, but the information may be valuable for the future. The credit union and the bank are the most usual providers of small personal loans. Investigate both of these sources.

Financial institution	Rates of interest	Conditions of approval

Hire purchase

Hire purchase is a form of credit. If you want to buy something and do not have the money for it, you can fill out what is called a credit clearance application form in the shop. The shop then sends this form to the bank. If the bank approves your application, it will pay the shop for the item and you pay the bank in instalments. Like most forms of credit, the interest rates are usually high and the item will cost you more, sometimes considerably more, than if you paid in full with cash. However, shops sometimes offer interest-free deals in a bid to get your custom. With hire purchase, you have use of the item, but do not officially own it until the last instalment is paid. So goods are not the property of the customer until the final payment is made. The customer will, however, have possession of the goods from day one.

EXAM TIME

Social Education (2007) – short questions

1. A guarantor for a loan is someone who:
   Agrees to pay part of the loan
   Provides a reference for the person taking out the loan
   Agrees to repay the loan if the borrower fails to repay the loan

2. Goods purchased on 'hire purchase' are:
   The property of the customer from the first payment
   Not given to the customer until after the final payment is made
   Not the property of the customer until the final payment is made

Social Education (2007) – long question

3. Words of Wisdom:
   A. Always read the small print
   B. Borrowing money costs money
   C. If you can't afford to save for it you can't afford to borrow for it

   (a) Select **one** of A, B, or C given above. Explain why this is valuable information for someone getting a loan. (Tick ✓ your choice.)

   Words of Wisdom   A   B   C

   Explain: _____

   (b) When taking out a loan a borrower is entitled to a ten-day 'cooling-off' period. What does this mean?

   _____
   _____

UNIT 5 Buying My Own Home

Mortgages

In the past only building societies offered mortgage loans. Nowadays, that market has widened to include banks, local authorities and life assurance companies. With so many different mortgage packages to choose from, the prospect of getting the right mortgage might seem a bit daunting. Competition of this sort, though, does mean a better deal for the consumer.

Applying for a mortgage

A mortgage is a loan that is given to you to buy property. The property is security for the loan and so you do not technically own your own home until the mortgage is paid in full. There are certain conditions attached to getting a mortgage. You must:

- be over 18 years of age
- be in secure employment
- have a sound financial history with no bad debts.

How much can I borrow?

- Because of dramatically rising house prices between about 1990 and 2007, lending institutions such as banks and building societies began lending greater amounts to borrowers than was the case in the past.
- In the past all mortgages required the borrower to have saved at least eight per cent of the house price as a deposit. During Ireland's economic boom, 100 per cent mortgages became available and no deposit was needed. Many economists felt that this was not good practice.
- In the past the amount that people were permitted to borrow was usually either twice or two and a half times their gross (before tax) annual salary. If they were buying the house with someone else the other person's salary was also added. Banks and building societies began lending four or five times annual salary as long as repayments did not exceed 40 per cent of the person's disposable income. This practice has now all but ceased.
- In the past the term for most mortgages was 20 to 25 years. Nowadays, however, terms can be for as long as 40 years. Because of all the interest paid, this is more expensive for the customer in the long run, but it means that actual monthly repayments will be less.
- Interest rates on mortgages can be either fixed or flexible. With fixed interest mortgages the same rate of interest is paid throughout the life of the mortgage (or sometimes a mortgage is fixed for a period of time during the mortgage). The advantage of fixed interest rate mortgages is that monthly repayments don't go up even if interest rates are raised by the Central Bank. The disadvantage is that often fixed interest rate

mortgages have relatively high rates of interest and the person can end up paying a lot more for their mortgage at times when interest rates are low.

Local authority mortgages

If you are unable to get a loan from a building society or bank, you may be eligible for a mortgage from your local authority.

The loan can be up to 97 per cent of the price of the house subject to a maximum loan of €185,000 and subject to repayments which are no more than 35 per cent of the household net income (i.e. income after tax and PRSI).

Special affordable housing mortgages were introduced by some commercial lenders towards the end of 2004. Rules vary but these mortgages generally offer up to 97 per cent of the purchase price and may not have maximum limits (unlike local authority loans, which are capped at €185,000). Applicants for private sector affordable mortgages must be pre-approved by their local authorities for a suitable property.

Rules

You may be eligible for a local authority mortgage if you can show the local authority that you cannot get a loan from a bank or building society and you are:

- In need of housing and your income satisfies the income test (see below).
- Registered on a housing waiting list with a local authority.
- A local authority tenant or a tenant purchaser and you want to buy a private house and return your present house to the local authority.
- A tenant for more than one year of a home provided by a voluntary body under the Capital Loan and Subsidy Scheme (previously known as the Rental Subsidy Scheme) and you want to buy a private house and return your present house to the local authority.

Note that the income test only applies to the first category; if you are covered by the second, third or fourth category you are exempt from the income test.

The income test

- **Single-income household** – if your gross income (before tax) in the last income tax year was €40,000 or less, you are eligible.
- **Two-income household** – Multiply the gross income (before tax) of the higher earner in the last income tax year by 2.5 and add the gross income of the other earner in the last income tax year. If the answer is €100,000 or less, you are eligible.

Compulsory Costs Involved in Buying a House

1. A deposit Usually eight per cent of the house price must be paid. Until recently 100 per cent mortgages were available for which no deposit was needed. Banks and building societies have stopped offering these mortgages.

2. An indemnity bond If you borrow more than 75 per cent of the house price, an indemnity bond (a form of insurance) is often required. Not all banks or building societies make this charge, so it is worth shopping around. It usually costs €150–€250.

3. A surveyor's report The building society or bank will send out a surveyor to make sure that the property is worth the money that they are lending you. You have to meet this cost. It is usually around €150. It is also advised that you get a structural survey done on the property. This survey will point out if there is anything wrong with the property, e.g. a roof that needs replacing.

4. Legal fees You will have to employ a solicitor, which usually costs up to one per cent of the house price. Some solicitors advertise an all-in-one fee which is the same regardless of the value of the house – usually around €1,500. Solicitors in urban areas (towns and cities) tend to be cheaper because of the greater competition.

5. Other fees In addition to his/her fee, the solicitor will charge search fees (€125), land registry fees (€350), deed registration (€65), and commissioners' fees (€25), making a total of €565 (approximate figures).

6. Stamp duty This is a government tax that must be paid on some new and second-hand houses. How much stamp duty (if any) you have to pay depends on four different factors:

    (a)   Whether you are a first-time buyer, an owner-occupier or an investor.

    (b)   Whether the house is new or second-hand.

    (c)   The size of the property.

    (d)   The value of the property.

New homes

- First-time buyers do not have to pay stamp duty on new homes.
- If the house is under 125 square metres owner-occupiers don't pay stamp duty either.
- Investors pay stamp duty in accordance with the table below regardless of house size.
- If a property is over 125 square metres the stamp duty is worked out as follows:

Property value	Rate
Up to €125,000	No stamp duty
Next €875,000	7%
Balance	9%

Second-hand homes

First-time buyers do not have to pay stamp duty on second-hand homes. Owner-occupiers and investors pay stamp duty at the following rates:

Property value	Rate
Up to €125,000	No stamp duty
Next €875,000	7%
Balance	9%

If someone is buying land or a site the amount of stamp duty paid is based solely on price – there is no reduction for first-time buyers or owner-occupiers. The amount of stamp duty paid ranges from zero per cent (land worth €10,000 or less) to nine per cent (if the land is worth over €150,000).

 **ACTIVITY**

Imagine you are a first-time buyer buying a second-hand house with an asking price of €200,000. How much in total will you have to pay? Will you have to pay stamp duty?

Some terms explained

Bridging finance/loan   A short-term loan to meet the cost of building or buying a new home while the borrower is awaiting the sale of the home he or she already owns. Most people dread this type of loan because of the high rates of interest that are charged.

Mortgage tax relief   If you have a mortgage, you are entitled to tax relief on the money you pay in interest. Tax relief is given at source, i.e. by your mortgage lender at the time the mortgage payment is made. This means that your mortgage payment is reduced by the amount of tax relief you are entitled to and your mortgage company then claims this back from the Revenue Commissioners. For a more detailed account of how mortgage relief works log onto www.revenue.ie.

Home improvement grants   Unless you live in a Gaeltacht area and therefore may be entitled to various home improvement grants, there are only a few government grants available. There is:

- A grant available for the repair of a thatched roof.
- An essential repairs grant available to elderly people, who would not be able to remain in their home if these repairs were not carried out.

If, however, you permanently reside in a Gaeltacht area or on one of the islands off our coast and Irish is the main language spoken at home, there are eight different types of grant that may be available to you. For further information on these grants contact the Department of Community, Rural and Gaeltacht Affairs. Tel: (091) 592555; Web: www.pobail.ie.

Main Steps Involved in Buying a House

 **ACTIVITY**

Below is a list of the twelve main steps involved in buying a house. Put the steps in the correct order by putting 1 in the box beside the first step, 2 beside the second step and so on.

Close sale.	
Pay fees.	
Check newspapers, estate agents ads, sales boards on actual houses.	
View properties within your price range.	
Employ a solicitor.	
Apply for a mortgage.	
Put a deposit on the house of your choice.	
Employ a surveyor to check the property over.	
Sign contracts.	
Move in.	
Ensure snag list is attended to by builder.	
Get mortgage approval.	

ACTIVITY

Go to a mortgage provider in your area. Ask them to give you details of the mortgage packages they have on offer. Ask them for a mortgage application form. Fill out this form using the following details:

The new house you are buying costs €249,000. You are married and you earn €44,000 per year and your partner earns €42,000.

1. What is the maximum you will be allowed to borrow?

   _____

2. How much money will you have to have for a deposit?

   _____

   Invent other likely details for the application form.
   Note: most banks and building societies will give you details of their mortgages on line.
   For example: www.bankingIreland.ie; www.ulsterbank.ie; www.firstactive.ie/mortgages;
   www.permanenttsb.ie.

ACTIVITY

Visit an estate agent's office and/or look in the property pages of local or national newspapers. Research your local housing market. Look at both new and second-hand houses in your area.
Find out the cost of each of:

1. A new, three-bedroom, semi-detached house.

   _____

2. A second-hand, three-bedroom, semi-detached house.

   _____

 **EXAM TIME**

Social Education (2005) – long question (part)

1. Climbing the property ladder may require:

- Mortgage protection
- Surveyor's report
- Stamp duty
- Secure employment

(a) Select **two** of the above requirements and explain each.

Requirement: _____

Explain: _____

Requirement: _____

Explain: _____

(b) What age must a person be in order to get a mortgage? _____

(c) What is a 90% mortgage? _____

_____

Social Education (2008) – long question (part)

2. 'Since March 31, 2007, stamp duty has been abolished for first-time buyers.'

Why is the abolition of stamp duty for first-time buyers good news for young people?

_____

_____

UNIT 6 Understanding Insurance

Some Definitions

Tick off each term if you understand it.

Premium

This is the amount of money your insurance policy costs you every year. You pay this to the insurance company.

No-claims bonus

You get a discount called a 'no-claims bonus' if you did not have any claims in the last year. With car insurance, to have a full no-claims bonus you need to have had three years' claim-free motoring.

Broker

A broker is a person who advises you on what insurance company suits your needs. He or she does not work for one particular insurance company and so will not be pushing one company on you even if it is not the best one for you. He/she is therefore in a position to give unbiased advice. If you take out a policy, the broker takes a commission.

Insurance agent

Unlike the broker, the insurance agent sells insurance for one company only, and will therefore be limited to their own products.

Insurance policy

This is the name given to the contract between you and the insurance company. It states what is covered, what premium you have to pay, etc.

Renewal notice

When your insurance policy is due for renewal, the insurance company will send you a reminder. This is called a renewal notice.

Loadings

When an insurance company gets an application for an insurance policy, it assesses that person in terms of risk. If you are a high-risk person, you have a high loading and your insurance will cost more. Young male drivers have a high loading and so can spend well in excess of €2,500 a year on car insurance.

Indemnity

This means that you cannot profit from an insurance claim. For example, you buy a car for €5,000 and in a year's time, when it is only worth €3,800, it is stolen and burned out. You can only claim €3,800, as that is all it was worth at the time.

Types of Insurance

There are various types of insurance that individuals or families may wish to have:

House insurance

This type of insurance covers both the actual building and its contents. In the event of fire or burglary, for example, the insurance company will compensate the owner.

Motor/car insurance

This type of insurance is required by law. Motor insurance can be third party; third party, fire and theft; or comprehensive. Third party means that the damage you do to another person or their vehicle is covered by the policy, but damage to you or your own vehicle is not.

Comprehensive insurance covers you and your own vehicle as well.

Mortgage protection   To get a mortgage you must have this type of insurance. If you have a mortgage and die before paying all of it off, the remainder of the mortgage is paid off by the insurance company.

Private health   You pay a premium to a health insurance company such as VHI or BUPA and, in the event of you becoming ill, you will receive private health care.

Personal accident insurance   This covers you if you had an accident and were unable to work.

Term life insurance   You insure your life for a fixed period of time, for example for twenty years while your children are young and unable to provide for themselves. If you do not die during this period, no compensation is paid out and there is no lump sum at the end of the term.

Holiday insurance   This type of insurance is taken out to compensate you for various difficulties that could occur while you are on holiday. Holiday insurance packages are all different, but usually cover items such as cancellations, medical emergency expenses, theft of personal property, delayed baggage, etc.

Assurance

So far we have looked at insurance. Insurance is paying money to a company so that they will compensate you if something happens, e.g. you become ill or have an accident. Assurance, on the other hand, which we will look at briefly now, pays out compensation for something that will happen, for example reaching the age of 65 or dying.

There are two main types of assurance:

Whole-life assurance   The policy holder pays a premium to the insurance company throughout their life. When the policy holder dies, compensation is paid to his or her next of kin.

Endowment life assurance   Compensation is paid out at a fixed age, usually 65. In the event of the policy holder dying before the stated age, the money is paid out then instead.

ACTIVITY

You have just bought a four-year-old Toyota Corolla (1.4L). You have recently passed your driving test. This is your first insurance policy. Fill out the motor insurance proposal form below. You will have to invent some details.

Proposal form for Private Motor Insurance

Section 1 – Proposers and Driver details

1. Full Name of Proposers

   2. Occupation

   Address

   3. Daytime phone number

4. Give details of all persons (including yourself) who will drive the vehicle:

Drivers			Driving Licence Details		
Name	DOB	Occupation	Relationship to you	Full or Provisional	How long is licence held?
Yourself					

5. To the best of your knowledge, have you or anyone else material to this policy ever: Yes No   If yes, give details

   (A) Been convicted of an offence or have one pending?

   (B) Had any claims against you in the last 5 years?

   (C) Been disqualified from driving?

   (D) Have defective vision, diabetes, suffer from fits or heart disease?

6. Have you or do you hold another insurance policy? If yes, state with which company and its expiry date.

7. Are you entitled to a no-claims bonus? (You will have to provide proof of this.)   How many years?

8. Are you or have you been a named driver on another policy? (If you have proof of this, you may be entitled to a discount.)   How many years?

9. Who will be the main driver of the car?

10. Would you like us to send you information on our house insurance policies?

Proposal form for Private Motor Insurance

Section 2 – Car details

Reg. No.	Make	Exact model, e.g.L, GI, Turbo, etc.	Cubic Capacity	Year of Manufacture	Present Value	Fuel

	Yes	No	If 'no', give details
Is the car owned and registered in your name?	☐	☐	
Is the car right-hand drive?	☐	☐	

	Yes	No	If 'yes', give details
Has the car been modified in any way?	☐	☐	
Will the car be used to pull trailers or caravans?	☐	☐	
Will the car be used for business other than driving to work?	☐	☐	

Declaration:

I, _____ confirm that all the details given on this form are to the best of my knowledge true.

Signed _____

Print name _____

Note: accurate quotes for motor and other forms of insurance are available over the phone.

⚙ ACTIVITY

Visit an insurance provider in your area. Gather forms, e.g. life, house or mortgage protection insurance. Practise filling in the forms.

Note: *How to settle a claim.* You must fill out a claim form and send it to your insurance company. The company then sends an assessor to inspect the damage and calculate compensation if it is to be paid. If you are claiming as a result of a burglary you will have to have a Garda report of the break-in.

EXAM TIME

Social Education (2005) – short questions

1. An insurance policy is:

   The contract between you and the insurance company

   The money you must pay to the insurance company

   The discount you receive for not having any claims in the last year

Social Education (2005) – long question (part)

2. Why is it important to take out holiday insurance?

   _____

   _____

Social Education (2006) – long question (part)

3. Your home has been burgled and a number of items have been stolen. Among the items taken are your TV and DVD player.

   Outline **three** steps you would take when making a claim to your insurance company for these items.

   1. _____

   2. _____

   3. _____

Social Education (2007) – long question (part)

4. Select **one** of the following insurance terms and explain what it means.

   Fully comprehensive

   Third party

   Premium

   No claims bonus

   Insurance term: _____

   Explain: _____

   _____

Social Education (2008) long question (part)

5. Name **one** type of insurance a young person is likely to purchase.

    Type of insurance: _____

    List **two** reasons why it is important to have this type of insurance cover.

    1. _____

    2. _____

2005 Leaving Certificate Applied Aural Examination

2006 Leaving Certificate Applied Aural Examination

2007 Leaving Certificate Applied Aural Examination

2008 Leaving Certificate Applied Aural Examination